A
CHINAMAN'S
CHANCE

Also by ERIC LIU

The Gardens of Democracy: A New Story of Citizenship, the Economy, and the Role of Government (with Nick Hanauer)

Imagination First (with Scott Noppe-Brandon)

The True Patriot (with Nick Hanauer)

Guiding Lights: How to Mentor—and Find Life's Purpose

The Accidental Asian: Notes of a Native Speaker

NEXT: Young American Writers on the New Generation (editor)

A CHINAMAN'S CHANCE

One FAMILY'S JOURNEY *and* *the* CHINESE AMERICAN DREAM

ERIC LIU

PUBLICAFFAIRS
NEW YORK

Published in the United States by PublicAffairs™,
a Member of the Perseus Books Group

Printed in the United States of America.

PublicAffairs books are available at special discounts for bulk purchases in the U.S. by corporations, institutions, and other organizations. For more information, please contact the Special Markets Department at the Perseus Books Group, 2300 Chestnut Street, Suite 200, Philadelphia, PA 19103, call (800) 810-4145, ext. 5000, or e-mail special.markets@perseusbooks.com.

Book design by Pauline Brown

Library of Congress Cataloging-in-Publication Data

Liu, Eric.

A Chinaman's chance : one family's journey and the Chinese American dream/ Eric Liu.

pages cm

Includes bibliographical references and index.

ISBN 978-1-61039-194-8 (hardcover)—ISBN 978-1-61039-195-5 (e-book) 1. Liu, Eric. 2. Chinese Americans—Biography. 3. Chinese Americans—Ethnic identity. 4. Chinese Americans—Cultural assimilation. 5. Children of immigrants—United States—Biography. 6. Parent and child—United States. 7. Chinese Americans—Languages. 8. United States—Race relations. I. Title. II. Title: One family's journey and the Chinese American dream.

E184.C5L622 2004

305.8951073—dc23

2014007474

First Edition

10 9 8 7 6 5 4 3 2 1

Contents

Prologue

MY FATHER, WHO HAD AN IRONIC SENSE OF HUMOR, took a certain delight from the phrase "a Chinaman's chance." People don't use that nineteenth-century expression anymore, but most of us still know what it means: no chance in hell. Dad sometimes liked to jest, about prosaic situations like getting to the store before closing, that neither he nor I had a Chinaman's chance. Of course, he tried hard all his life here to prove that saying wrong. So have I. So have nearly four million Chinese Americans.

The Census tells us that Chinese Americans today have among the highest incomes and highest levels of education of any ethnic group in America. Our senses tell us that there is more to the picture. There are Chinese American stories of striving and struggle that don't fit the box of a government form or the narrative of the model minority, from families who've been here many generations to lone migrants who arrived yesterday. And the gleaming promise and looming menace of modern China *colors* the perception of people who look like me—and indeed colors our own self-perceptions.

The great American kaleidoscope of migration and acculturation, the tumbling fractal dance of colors colliding, of fusion and diffusion, has turned for over a century and a half for the Chinese of America. With each generation we have changed this country—its laws and voice and palate and face. The kaleidoscope gyrates still, but now in a world where the Chinese of China also have something to say about what it is to matter and to have influence and to be *seen*.

What does it mean to be Chinese American in this moment of China and America? It means being a vessel for all the anxieties and hopes that attend the arrival of China on the world scene. It means creating a new template for American immigrant arrival—the Chinese cannot be reduced to new Jews; the history of the Chinese in America is unique, and richer than most know. It means being a test case for some of the great questions of our day: Does Chinese culture somehow confer a competitive advantage? Is it possible for America, the planet's most efficient hybridizer of cultures, to capitalize fully on the talents and passions and character of those of us of Chinese ancestry?

Here, in thc pages to follow, are the reflections of one Chinaman on chance: on the role of chance in his own family's journey, and on the chance America still has to be something greater than the sum of its many tinted parts.

CHAPTER 1

What Confucius Didn't Say

The Master said, "At fifteen, I set my heart on learning; at thirty I took my stand; at forty I came to be free of doubts; at fifty I understood the Decree of Heaven; at sixty my ear was attuned; at seventy I followed my heart's desire without overstepping the line."

THIS PASSAGE FROM *THE ANALECTS* OF CONFUCIUS (Book II.4) has always stirred in me a mix of aspiration and anxiety—the aspiration to seek ever-greater wisdom; the anxiety of not feeling quite age-appropriately wise. A kind of ethical clock ticks loudly in my brain whenever I read these words of the Master. They remind me of the passage from Ben Franklin's *Autobiography* in which he describes himself at age twenty making a list of personal virtues (temperance, frugality, cleanliness, humility, and so forth) and keeping a daily chart of his adherence to each. I didn't discover Franklin's regimen of structured self-improvement until I was well into my thirties. The discovery led me both to push myself and to kick myself: *I ought to be more like that—but it's too late to become like that!*

I am now forty-five. I am not yet free of doubts. In five years I am supposed to understand the Decree of Heaven. I confess to you I do not know the Decree and cannot claim to have mastered it. I do know, however, that the Chinese term for Decree of Heaven—*tian ming*—translates more accurately to "heavenly fate." And I am beginning, maybe right on schedule, to appreciate the meaning of fate.

"Fate" is another word for "the die is cast." Fate is a set of patterns 99 percent unseen and only 1 percent within our ken—and it's that tantalizing 1 percent that generates our entire sense of free will and of personal responsibility to make or remake ourselves, to change or fulfill our destiny. Perhaps 99/1 is the wrong split. Maybe it's 80/20. Or 51/49. I am not yet free of doubts. But I am old enough now, and have moments enough of wisdom, to realize that many forces unseen and unwitting have bent the strange loop of my identity: my ways of seeing people, refracting the light of situations, facing history, dreaming. For so many years I have imagined myself as the author of my own story. I have imagined identity to be a matter simply of what I *choose* to identify with. Like so many Americans, I have cherished the liberty of such choice.

I had to claim it early. When my father died, we both were too young. He was fifty-four and I twenty-two. I had no choice but to choose my own way, to start crafting a story of self and place with what I had at hand. And I came to imagine that anything at hand must have been of my own making. Like so many Americans, I imagined myself self-made. But today I stand more than two decades from the death of my father, and fifteen years into fatherhood myself. And now I see myself more clearly: not as the author solely, or even primarily, but more as the page; less the calligrapher than the parchment, absorbing the ink and scripts of others.

When she was eleven, my daughter, Olivia, decided it would be amusing to make up sayings by Confucius. She scribbled on a sheet of loose-leaf paper, giggling as she wrote, leaving chunks of hurried script that looked like graffiti or furtive notes to a classmate:

> *Birds must live off the bird feeder to survive the harsh winter. I know this because I've seen it happen with my own two buggy eyes.*
>
> —Confucius

> *Simply Xerox.*
>
> —Confucius

> *Confucius does not like to look in the mirror and see any man but Confucius.*
>
> —Confucius

> *If you want a flower to grow, you must wait until springtime, for that is when I talk to the bears around me.*
>
> —Confucius

> *In your pocket, there is pocket lint.*
>
> —Confucius

To have tossed off such absurdities—they read like the comedic tweets of someone with the handle @FakeConfucius—she must have come into contact at some point with Confucian epigrams and then later with the fortune-cookie bastardizations of those epigrams. Perhaps she saw, as I once saw when I was her age, a white person on TV or in the hallway at school squint his eyes, fold his mouth into an obsequious grin, and utter in a fake accent and broken English: "Confucius sayyyy. . . ." She must have absorbed the American notion that to be Chinese is to be wise, often inscrutably, and profound, often misleadingly. She must also have picked up on the idea that to be Chinese American in the twenty-first century is to be able to make fun of it all—the Chinese, the Americans, the pictures each has of the other, the eminently laughable self-seriousness of anyone advertised as a "Master," the earnestness of people (like her father) who seek insight from Masters. But where and when these patterns of thought took hold in her I can't say.

Actually, I can—to an extent. Her scribblings poured forth one afternoon when we were sitting at our kitchen nook and she was trying to avoid the weekly Chinese tutorial I give her. I have a pretty high tolerance for her evasions, especially when they are creative, so I went along. After every few of the parody maxims she wrote, I'd add one:

> *I forgot where I put my toast.*
>
> —Confucius

> *What did you say?*
>
> —Confucius

> *Do you have change for a dollar?*
>
> —Confucius

Mine were not as inspired or spontaneous as hers. But they turned her playfulness into a game for us both. To play at being Chinese is, I sometimes think, the most I will be able to do. I don't mean that entirely self-damningly. I have not attained mastery of my cultural inheritance. I remain half-proficient in Chinese conversation, able to understand more than I am able to express. I am half-proficient in Chinese history and ethics and art, not insensate but not fully discerning.

Still, my partial knowledge is greater than that of many ABCs (American-born Chinese, as we of the second generation are sometimes called). I am definitely conveying to Olivia the core elements of the language and the sensibility that hides inside the valence of each character and each grammatical convention. She knows that the translation of an English sentence like "Why did you teach me this today?" is, roughly, "You today why teach me this?" And she senses that this order has meaning, that the logic is not just syntactic but also relational: start with the other person, the larger context. It's enough to fashion something. With a little ingenuity and a spark of improvisation, I may still be able to ignite in my daughter a sense that within our games and our intermittent tutorials and her irreverent appropriations of other people's appropriations of Confucius are the faint outlines of a civilization.

> The Master said, "I never enlighten anyone who has not been driven to distraction by trying to understand a difficulty or who has not got into a frenzy trying to put his ideas into words. When I have pointed out one corner of a square to someone and he does not come back with the other three, I will not point it out to him a second time." (Book VII.8)

In recent months I have begun reading *The Analects* with my mother. Julia Liu was born in Nanjing in 1937, the year of the Rape of Nanjing, though by the time of those atrocities she and her family had already moved on to another city. Her father was a reformist professor of European history, part of the idealistic "May 4 generation" that, fed up with the backwardness and weakness of imperial China, took to the streets in protest on May 4, 1919. Her mother was a restless young student of that professor. Their marriage came at a time when nearly every social and political tradition in China was collapsing, but it displeased both their families so much that they essentially were left on their own. Their tiny family lived an itinerant life, ranging across a landscape of war and upheaval, going wherever there were enough people, and enough stability, to support a university.

Because Japanese and later Communist Chinese troops seemed always to be approaching, they kept moving across China, to Xian to Chenggu to Lanzhou and ultimately, after the Communist victory on the mainland, to Taipei. At home—wherever that was at any given moment—my mother heard her father rail against the stultifying legacy of Confucianism, the suffocating formats of Chinese education. His influence seeped into her childhood imagination. Far more compelling to her than the classical Chinese legends of "The Monkey King" or "The Journey to the West" were romantic tales from the actual West: *Wuthering Heights* and the novels of Turgenev and the other great Russians, all in translation.

So it is that only in recent years, in her seventies, is she doing her first truly close reading of some of the canonical Chinese texts. She has a group of dear friends, all living in the suburbs of Washington, DC—all, remarkably, alumnae of the same middle school in Taipei—who call themselves the Bon Sisters. The Bon Sisters go to galleries and concerts and parties together. Mom also has a book club with other Chinese friends, and lately they've been working their way through the great texts of the Confucian age.

I read Confucius, in English, when I was a junior at Yale. It was one of the required texts for Modern Chinese History, the survey course taught by the erudite and eloquent Jonathan Spence. He was finishing his book *The Search for Modern China* that semester, and each week in class we got to read chapters of his typed manuscript, with scribbled edits in the margins. But that meant he never got to go deep with us on *The Analects*.

In my untutored reading as a twenty-year-old the translation struck me as mystifyingly vague or simply banal. The precepts of the Master had neither the crisp utility of Sun Tzu's *Art of War* ("If your opponent is of choleric temper, irritate him") nor the inspirational quality of, say, Proverbs of the King James Bible. Instead, it was filled with lines that left me cold:

> The Master said, "Is one who simply sides with tenacious opinions a gentleman? Or is he merely putting on a dignified appearance?" (Book XI.21)

I could perceive, dimly, that there was more to a line like that than a first reading might suggest. "Gentleman," for instance, is a concept that comes up over and over. To a native reader of English, the word connotes nobility or gracious formality. The word used in *The Analects*, though, is *junzi*, for which "gentleman" is really an inadequate translation. "Honorable person" or "moral one" comes closer but still misses the mark, or smudges it. Really, the best way to express *junzi* is just *junzi*, in the way that *machismo* is simply *machismo*. A second-degree equivalent, like "masculine bluster," just doesn't quite capture it. This gap, between "gentleman" and *junzi*, reveals how even a universal moral sensibility has to be expressed in the particulars of one culture or another. It reveals too the asymptotically frustrating nature of translation, which can bring you ever closer, but never quite all the way, to the original line. At the time, though, none of this captured my imagination. I was quite uninterested in looking for the other corners of the square. I thought that any translation that used "gentleman" so frequently, that put such a core Chinese idea into such ill-fitting Anglo clothing, must be inherently flawed and not worth taking very seriously.

Now I've returned to the text, newly attentive. My mother and I have made reading Confucius a weekly ritual, and our painstaking bilingual method has many steps. First, I choose some passages in English that intrigue me, from my Penguin paperback. After she's had some time to look up those passages in her Chinese edition, she gets me on speakerphone. She begins by reading the passages in the original, a high-literary, archaic form of Chinese. In this form, Confucius is not intelligible to me. But then she "translates" that classical Chinese into more contemporary and colloquial Chinese (so-called *baihua*, or "plain white language"). I understand better. Next, she tries her best to translate the *baihua* version into English. Then I compare her English translation with that of the Penguin edition, published in 1979 (before Deng Xiaoping had set China on the course of renewal) by a Hong Kong academic named D. C. Lau. Along the way, each of us might consult Google Translate—she entering a Chinese character into the text box, I from the other direction. It's all pretty nerdy.

One afternoon we started our study session with the famous passage at the start of this chapter ("At fifteen, I set my heart on learning . . ."). My mom herself had probably been about fifteen when she'd first learned this passage, but it had bounced off her then as yet another Confucian cliché in a boring textbook. Now she appreciates it, at least the parts about being sixty and seventy. Her ear seems attuned. She seems to follow her heart's desire without ever overstepping the line. She always has been intuitive—my father, by comparison, was the one with the analytical bent. Today, though, my mother's intuition has been honed into a full-field awareness, a sense of simple confluence with the laws of nature—which, incidentally, is how she prefers to translate *tian ming*, the Decree of Heaven. "I just feel I'm *with* life now" is how she puts it. She adds: "I go through a lot of happiness and tragedy."

My father died in 1991. But what my mother talks about today is not how short his life was or long hers has been without him. She talks of their courtship. She'd had two suitors, Dad and another guy. The other guy was the one her parents preferred. She was torn. She told both that she had to cut things off. And as soon as she did, two things became clear to her: first, she didn't care about ending things with the other guy, and second, when she imagined not being with Dad, she felt "the sky was falling."

> The Master said, "There is nothing I can do with a man who is not constantly saying, 'What am I to do? What am I to do?'" (Book XV.16)

In the Chinese original, this sentence is inverted:

> The Master said, "The man who doesn't ever say, 'What am I to do? What am I to do?'—there's nothing I can do with him."

I much prefer this original structure. The translation flips it for simplicity, but in the flip is lost the spirit, the intention, the making into an object lesson of that unquestioning, unreflective guy. Of course, in any language, with any inflection, there are still many ways to read "What am I to do? What am I to do?" Is it an expression of indecision, of ambivalence among too many options? Is it helplessness in the face of calamity? Is it inquisitiveness about motives and morals? Pure existentialism? A yowl of futility? In Mom's interpretation, this passage is simply a brief for deliberateness, for thinking clearly about a situation and not being *shuibian*—"any which way," "careless"—about it. My interpretation pushes further. To me, this passage is essentially the Chinese equivalent of the Socratic claim that the unexamined life is not worth living. It has exactly the same rhetorical assertiveness and moral severity: the unexamined life is not just less good; it's *useless*. To me, Socrates's statement would have been the ideal "translation" of the Confucian original. For translation is not primarily about lining up each word of one language into a decoded word of another; it is primarily about conveying the essence of meaning.

Meaning, though, changes with time; text with context. *What am I to do?* There was a time, as in the minutes after we learned of my father's death, when those words or words roughly like them, uttered in panic, escaped my mother's lips. Today, after so many years of lonely meditation, and so many conversations with me that describe but a fraction of those meditations, and so many outings and travels with her Bon Sisters and other friends to explore beyond those meditations, my mother says the words with new meaning. Today she asks the question with what Zen Buddhists call "beginner's mind." A lack of preconception, a reflexive resistance to rutted thinking. A life-sustaining curiosity that takes each moment as a fresh start. *What am I to do?* has become, for my seventy-seven-year-old mother, *What might I do?*

I have now lived more of my life without my father than with him. "Unexpectedly" was the adverb we attached to his death in the days immediately after the fact. I wrote it into his obituary. And it's true: the actual moment of his passing, sometime in the deep dark before dawn on July 8, 1991, was indeed not expected. But the *possibility* of it had loomed over us for many years. In that sense the arrival of the ultimate moment had been long expected, long dreaded, long kept at bay in the fringes of my imagination.

In the years that have since passed, the classic quest for substitute fathers hasn't really been my thing. Instead I have quested for insight, for some grand unified theory of cause and effect and the nature of suffering that could make sense of this riddle: how my father's last moments could be so unexpected when I'd spent all that time anticipating them. I've hoped such a revelation might make life seem less random, or at least more comprehensibly random. That's why I bring a certain interpretation to Confucian precepts like this:

> The Master said, "In instruction there is no separation into categories." (Book XV.39)

In English that sentence seems graceful and compact. But consider the Chinese original: *You jiao wu lei.* "Have teaching no category." *That's* compact. That explosive concision, that charged latent space between ideas that requires a reader or listener to ignite each word's full meaning, is the hallmark of the Chinese language. It is also the hallmark of poetry, in which, the dictionary tells us, "special intensity is given to the expression of feelings and ideas by the use of distinctive style and rhythm." It's the reason why Chinese is inherently more poetic than English.

When I first encountered this line, I read it as a cosmic statement about the ethics of interdependence, about how we are webbed into a vast matrix of circumstance and choice and accident. I read it as the Eastern rebuke to the Western obsession with classification and breaking things down into artificial chunks. Our lives are entwined. Karma circulates without end and without regard for our feeble attempts to locate or direct it. There's no splitting your misfortune off from my good fortune. There is no converting the harmful effects of my actions into what economists call "externalities." There is no such thing as externalities. All costs and errors and harms are always, eventually, internalized. There is no separation into categories.

Moreover, I filled in the blanks of *You jiao wu lei* by interpreting *lei* to mean "categories of learning." I took it to say that to study at any level of seriousness the student must ignore the disciplinary borderlines between sociology and psychology and history and physics and biology—because they are all the same thing. They are all variations on the theme of how complex adaptive living systems—gardens, rivers, the body—operate. It was thrilling to come upon an axiom that captured my way of thinking about thinking.

Only it turns out my reading was wrong. The *baihua* version, like Talmudic commentary, explains that the categories in question are not categories of learning but categories of *learners*: whether a learner is rich or poor, from a royal or a common family. These categories of status should not matter, Confucius is saying; learning is learning, and teaching is teaching. It is an admirable, even democratic, conception of the universal leveling power of education. To my mother, this meaning was obvious. But I insisted on the plausibility of my alternate reading. She refused to acknowledge it. She got a little exercised about it, in fact, as if I were insisting that blue was red.

The difference was simply this: she had background knowledge about how this axiom was taught in China, about how people talked about it in China, about the larger idea of education that it implied; I did not. She read context into the text. I did not. But was my lack of context really a disadvantage? I saw simply an English translation that was ambiguous as to categories and a Chinese original that was as opaque as a koan. I read the calligraphic characters—which are, after all, just a specific type of inkblot—a certain way. My way. Isn't every translation, in the end, a Rorschach test? A translator's job is inherently impossible: no matter how carefully he chooses his words, he can never know what meaning will alight in the reader's mind. To be Chinese American is to sense this quantum overlay of possible connotations, interpretations, and identities. No separation into categories.

China is particularly prone to viruses. Bird flu and H1N1, yes. But also the social variety: memes that "go viral" into mass behavioral phenomena. That was how the Cultural Revolution, with its contagious frenzies of purification and purge, came to pass. Today, amid the relentless centrifugal force of market capitalism—the true cultural revolution—1.3 billion Chinese yearn primally for something to hold them together, a useable past that points an ethical way to the future. Which is why in recent years China has fallen in love with Confucius. That might sound odd, but in fact the twentieth century—from the republican overthrow of dynastic rule to the arrival of history-obliterating Communism—had all but shoved Confucius into oblivion in China. He stood for backwardness, for a past that had to be shed.

Then in 2006, CCTV, China's state-owned television network, broadcast a weeklong series on the teachings of Confucius. It became an immediate and unexpected sensation. Yu Dan, an unassuming lecturer from Beijing Normal University, published a book based on the series called *Confucius from the Heart*, and she became a celebrity. The book has sold well over ten million copies (although, the English preface notes, matter-of-factly, that over six million were pirated). Today, a Confucius revival is in full swing across China. Old temples have been refurbished, old teachings re-esteemed. A statue of Confucius was installed outside Tiananmen Square. Political leaders now cite the old Master more often than they quote Mao. China's soft-power diplomacy has also been shaped by the revival: the Chinese government has partnered with universities across the United States and other countries to establish "Confucius Institutes" that introduce the basics of Chinese culture to foreigners.

There was a time, of course, when people blamed Confucianism for China's backwardness. The sociologist Max Weber wrote in 1915 that Confucian ethics were so bound to social class and the status quo, and so focused on ritualism and ancestor worship, that China was inherently unable to adapt to the challenges and threats of a changing world. This was his explanation for why capitalism had never taken root in China and, implicitly, how a great civilization had devolved into an ungovernable mess. His explanation became conventional wisdom in the West—and among Chinese reformers like my mother's father. Today, though, Confucianism is cited as a driving force for China's meteoric resurgence. Now it is used to explain why capitalism *has* taken root in China and flowered beyond imagining, and how China *has* been able to harness its entropy into single-minded action. The dedication, the rigor, the self-sacrifice needed to make family and nation great, the profound reverence for learning—all these elements of China's economic miracle are now described as elements of the Confucian legacy.

How to resolve this discrepancy? One approach is to say that if one of these readings of history is true, the other cannot be: Confucianism is either harmful or helpful. Another is to assume that Confucianism is of only secondary relevance: it was not the driver of either China's long stagnation or its renaissance, and any assertion to the contrary is just ex post facto justification by each era's winners. But most plausible is the notion that both readings are true: Confucianism has caused, at different times, both the stagnation and the revitalization of China.

In fact, it may have caused them at the *same* time. In America, freedom liberates and oppresses: it removes limitations, but it creates the enormous burden of living with others who have no limits. In China, obligation—for that is, in the end, what Confucianism boils down to—similarly frees and confines. In a Chinese American heart, all this is combined. It is from this cross-grained weave of liberty and duty that a Chinese American life gets its integrity—and its tension.

Confucianism is sometimes called a religion, but it's not, exactly. It has a moral code and a foundational emphasis on the Golden Rule. But it is not institutionalized. It has spiritualism but no god. It's concerned, rather, with the spirit of belonging and interdependence that social animals like us feel—what in most translations of *The Analects* is called "benevolence."

Like "gentleman," this word in English has a whiff of noblesse oblige. In the language of Western philosophy, benevolence is *supererogatory*: not an obligation but an act of charity beyond the call of duty. But to be properly Confucian is to see acts like piety toward elders and ancestors not as beyond the call but *as* the call. It is our duty to contribute to the maintenance of a healthy society; our duty calls us to a way of being that's unsatisfyingly translated as "benevolence."

The scholar Tu Wei-ming spent a lifetime teaching at Harvard and now in elderhood has returned to Beijing. A native of China, he writes in English masterfully. Tu acknowledges the many ways that Confucian ideals, as they ossified into practice across the millennia, helped shape a toxic feudal Chinese culture of "authoritarianism, paternalism, ritualism, collectivism, nepotism, particularism, and male-domination." But he believes there is a baby to rescue from this fouled bathwater, a "new Confucian humanism" that melds the best of Confucianism with the best of Enlightenment values—and also excises the worst of each. If Confucianism is guilty of ratifying stasis, Enlightenment values are oblivious to their own hubris and self-centeredness. The "living Confucian," Tu writes, "cannot take for granted that the Confucian message is self-evidently true." He must humbly search out the meaning anew, to cultivate his own knowledge. Nor does the idea of such learning for the sake of self ever mean "a quest for one's individuality." Self, in Tu's interpretation of the Confucian canon, is inherently relational and communal.

Reading the supple, nuanced, and painstaking distinctions and syntheses of Tu Wei-ming, one quickly appreciates the brittle and tinny quality of China's contemporary Confucian revival. *Confucius from the Heart* reads as if it were a Chinese knockoff of a second-rate American self-help book, translated back into very basic English. It reduces *The Analects* into *Egg Drop Soup for the Soul*, a pop guide for dealing with anxiety, stress, disappointment, isolation—the pathologies of a culture dealing for the first time with individualism on a mass scale and unfettered individual ambition and materialism. It implies that the Chinese mind today, bewildered by change and unsure of any cosmology but greed, is in need of a crutch and, indeed, has come to mistake the crutch for a limb.

Yet I've watched this Confucian revival in China with great interest. I don't judge too harshly the crude remedies being offered and grasped at—not only because I have an intellectual interest but also because I understand, and indeed share, the yearnings. I too have sought a purpose to guide me through a tradition-smashing maelstrom. In my case, that maelstrom is American life.

Second-generation American life in particular. The child of immigrants is the purest embodiment of the contradictions of America. In that son or daughter—who, no matter how old, will always first be a son or daughter—is the sensation of perpetually wondering whether one's true self is somewhere else. To Americanize is to shed and to accumulate, to wipe the past away and to frantically try to satiate a hunger for memory. The first generation—my mother and my father—had to contend with their own forms of loss, but by the time they came to America they had deep foundations of Chineseness. The third generation—my daughter—has intermittent experiences of what W. E. B. DuBois called the "double consciousness" of minority identity. But in the second generation, my generation, the doubling is ubiquitous. Faith in something lasting, an original creed, is precious. And elusive.

I've realized lately how devoid of rites my life has been. The first time I ever bowed three times to honor a dead ancestor was at my father's funeral. I did it only because other people were doing it. It was the first time I'd witnessed these people I knew—family friends, my uncle, my mother—doing it. Now, whenever I visit my father's grave, I always end my silent, tearful visit with three bows, the last one deepest and held for a beat longer than the first two. I bow even though no one is looking. I do not visit my father as often as the rites say I should. When I arrive, I sweep and polish his grave and flat bronze memorial marker—his "spirit-tablet," as the Confucian texts call it—pulling at strands of grass that threaten to encroach the clean border of marble. His grave sits on a hill facing a tree and a river—the wide silent Hudson, far enough upstream that it seems as still as a lake. To sit here is to contemplate the unceasing current beneath the stillness. It is to find in nature what the rites were meant to make a person embody.

When I was a boy and my father was sick, I did not have prayer or church or the organized comforts of a faith tradition. The first time my father was hospitalized, my mother encouraged my sister and me to pray. We found an old Bible with a thin, flimsy black leather cover that looked as if it had been used by itinerant preachers a century earlier. I still do not know where it came from. But the Good Book was as bewildering to me then as *The Analects* would be later. It gave no guidance about how to pray in this situation, what to say in the midst of this crisis. So my mother—brave and, I realize now, so young—simply encouraged us to make up our own prayers—"Pray God take care of Daddy"—and we prayed together silently.

It didn't feel sufficient. I began privately to devise my own ritual, my own convoluted ways to ward off the badness. I would refine it in the weeks and months and years ahead. There was a certain doorway where I'd stood when I'd learned my father was in the hospital, and so in that doorway I would stand when no one else was around, facing the jamb, getting right up close to it, and letting a deeply private obsessive-compulsive liturgy unfold: counting tiny steps to and fro, muttering in Chinglish, praying to a kind of god with whom I had no acquaintance, slapping my own cheek periodically to banish dark thoughts of death, inhaling and sighing. And when my father recovered that first time, it confirmed that these rites I had invented had worked. And so I continued them, prophylactically, to keep my father alive. This was my expression of filial piety. It was an autodidact's hodgepodge prayer, with all the sincerity and hybrid incoherence of the self-taught. It was superstition and fear speaking a pidgin tongue of hope and devotion. It was my Chinese American prayer.

I ask Chinese Americans, especially others of the second generation, what makes them Chinese. They have many answers. No one ever mentions Confucianism. The closest they come is to speak of respect for elders and an acute awareness of social hierarchies. Otherwise, when they describe how they are Chinese, they speak of having social styles that are "more blunt and, um, 'efficient' (?) than white Americans." Or of "the ability to play at Chinese one-downmanship," that reflexive minimization of one's own accomplishments, especially in the company of other Chinese Americans. They speak of cravings for Chinese food. They speak of red envelopes and hot pot on special occasions. Mainly, though, they speak of difference, of being constantly reminded of the condition of not being white: "My name," says one, is what it means to be Chinese; "My slight accent," says another. They speak of being anointed as representatives of their race, marked as the point from which white schoolmates and neighbors could extrapolate a fuller picture of Chineseness.

But there is more.

David Hackett Fischer, the historian of American political culture, wrote a book that has deeply influenced how I see myself and immigrants and the children of immigrants. *Albion's Seed* describes in fascinating detail how colonists from four distinct regions of Great Britain bequeathed to what would become the United States four very different regional folkways. Thus a thread of righteous, reticent, self-leveling Puritanism runs across the upper continent from Boston to Minneapolis to Seattle. An aggrieved underdog Scotch-Irish streak is marbled throughout Appalachia. The hierarchical, honor-obsessed pride and prejudice of royalist Cavaliers was passed to the plantation South. An egalitarian pluralism was carried by the Quakers into the Delaware Valley. As much as our nation's culture is marked today by homogenized McFranchises, there remain all around us vestigial and sometimes fully expressed forms of these and other distinct lines of ethnocultural descent.

So it is that most Chinese Americans I know, even in our assimilated lives, operate with a stronger-than-average sense of rite, propriety, social context, and obligation. To look closely at the attitudes and behaviors of all those who protested that their lapsed Chineseness amounted only to a taste for hot pot is to discern the persistent influence of Confucian culture in a hundred ways. When we were children, we were praised for *dongshi* ("understanding things," "having social judgment") or scolded for being *meiyouyong* ("of no use to others"). Our grandmothers nodded approvingly when we addressed them in the proper tone and formal second person: "*Ta hao you limao*," they'd say to our parents—"he is so polite" or, more literally, "he so has politeness." We heard the tone of scorn in phrases like *diulian* and *buyaolian*—"throwing away face," "rejecting face"—that conveyed the worst of all social crimes: insufficient regard for the regard of others. We understood that *jia*—family—was an enclosed sphere around which other parts of society orbited.

But Chinese Americans of the second generation or beyond are not, even in the most isolated ethnic enclaves, simply good Chinese boys and girls transplanted whole into the American heartland. Our form of Confucian ethics has mutated: attenuated in some places, enlarged in others. The environment has forced the mutations.

Consider Maya Lin. She took her stand early, at twenty, when her design for the Vietnam Memorial was selected and she withstood a storm of criticism from veterans and politicians. She is an icon now. She towers above other public artists, not in the performance-art manner of a dissident among sheep like Ai Wei Wei, but in a disciplined and quiet way—a Way, as Confucius would say—that recalls Chinese landscape painters a millennium ago. Her father, an immigrant from China, was a ceramicist at Ohio State University. His aesthetic was Chinese and Japanese. His openness to letting young Maya explore and tinker in his workshop was American. And though in childhood she rarely contemplated her Chineseness—"I grew up almost oblivious to my Asian heritage," she writes—she has become "increasingly conscious of how my work balances and combines aspects of my Eastern and Western heritages." In her book *Boundaries*, Lin gives a succinct statement of purpose: "Each of my works originates from a simple desire to make people aware of their surroundings, not just the physical world but also the psychological world we live in."

There is something spiritual in this, but as with Taoism or Confucianism the spirit is humanist. The gods are not in the picture. It is for us, the living, to dedicate ourselves. Her acts of creation mark her as a fearless individual. Her works, from the Vietnam Memorial in Washington to the Civil Rights Memorial in Alabama to the Langston Hughes Library in Tennessee, situate her in the psychological world of America. People like Maya Lin have managed to hold on to the most beneficial parts of the Confucian meme even as they have absorbed the most vital and exceptional strands of the American. This is evolution, but it is *intelligent* evolution—not the result of impersonal genetic algorithms that weed out unfitness and spit out survivors, but the result of a cultivated intention to splice, synthesize, and preserve the most adaptive traits for another generation. To design. To make original hybrids—seeds not only of Albion but also of Cathay and many points between.

When you grow up Chinese American, you sometimes surprise yourself by how you unconsciously filter everyday experience through a Chinese screen. When I was eight or nine, my comprehension of Abbott and Costello's "Who's on First?" routine was impeded by my assumption that they were saying, "Hu's on First." I'd just learned to play baseball, so it made sense that another Chinese guy, someone named Hu, would be in the game. How that connected to the rest of what seemed to be the joke I couldn't tell. Subtler is when my daughter, Olivia, began to address my partner, Jená, by Jená's childhood nickname, Nay Nay. Except that Olivia, who would've been seven or so and had just started learning the pinyin transliterations of Chinese words into English, automatically spelled it "Nei Nei."

I remember as a teenager in the 1980s listening with pricked-up ears to the pop-punk song "Turning Japanese": "I think I'm turning Japanese, I think I'm turning Japanese, I really think so." I listened for racism in those lyrics or the voices (and didn't find any). I listened for racism in the way others, even my friends, listened to and resang the song (and didn't find any). I listened for people who might want to inject a random mutation into the song and start singing, "I think I'm turning Chi-i-nese, I think I'm turning Chi-i-nese, I really think so" (and didn't find any). Such was the vigilance of the minority boy, ever on the lookout for hints of ethnic hostility.

But it turns out that in the second decade of the second millennium of the Common Era, Americans are *really* turning Chinese. People without my ten thousand generations of black-haired Chinese genes are running more of the flow of their everyday lives through Chinese filters. There is the material of popular culture: *feng shui* consultants, *qi gong* classes, mu shu pork burritos, and so forth. But beneath these are deeper patterns of thought. In medicine, crime prevention, technology and new media, education, urban planning, business leadership, and parenting, a new language is coming to the fore. It's a relational language, a language of context and webs of social norms. It's a language of holism that transcends rugged individualism and adds a horizontal axis to the vertical mode of American striving.

And it's not just among liberals and ex-hippies that this awareness of holism has come to the fore. Consider a book that has sold as well in the United States as *Confucius from the Heart* has in China: Rick Warren's *The Purpose-Driven Life.* That book, by the evangelical minister of an Orange County megachurch, uses the language of Christianity the way Yu Dan uses the language of Confucius: to remind us that we are part of something greater than ourselves. The first line of Warren's book: "It's not about you."

Is there a less American-sounding sentence? The fact that tens of millions of American believers of all races and backgrounds have hungered to be told this suggests to me that we are in the early days of a great synthesis. What will the fusion of East and West look like? It will take a myriad of forms. Most important among them will be shifts in imagination: new stories we imagine for this nation. In another book I have argued that great citizenship means recognizing that "society becomes how you behave"—that there is no way to rationalize one's bad acts with the assumption that they'll be balanced by someone else's good acts; that if you choose to become more civil or courteous or compassionate, or less, you set off a contagion that makes society that much more all those things, or less. When I wrote those words, I realized that I was expressing a Confucian truth.

It was a revelation, just as the character-by-character excavation of *The Analects* with my mother has shown me all the ways that, in spite of her upbringing and mine, I am deeply Confucian. I am oriented toward duties, I think about webs of relationship and obligation, and I think of life itself as a demand for constant self-cultivation. Yet, situated in America, I have come to express this Confucianism in the language of the American creed. I speak of liberty as responsibility. I read Adam Smith not for *The Wealth of Nations*, which was co-opted a century later to justify laissez-faire capitalism, but for his *Theory of Moral Sentiments*, which reminded readers that no market can last without trust, cooperation, mutuality, reciprocity, and the social virtues. I assert a vision of patriotism in America that's more about barn raisings and D-Day than about rugged individualism and lone cowboys.

All this represents more than just the ethical wish fulfillment of one Chinese American. It also restates a forgotten foundation of American identity. In *Inventing America*, the historian Garry Wills applies to the Declaration of Independence the same method of textual deconstruction that he later applied to the

Gettysburg Address in *Lincoln at Gettysburg. Inventing America* describes how several thinkers of the Scottish Enlightenment—Adam Smith, David Hume, and, even more, the lesser-known Francis Hutcheson—shaped Thomas Jefferson's patterns of thought and infused in the words of the Declaration a coherent and truly revolutionary moral vision. The vision, now undetectable to most Americans, was this: every right is a duty. Wills puts it thus:

> Life and liberty are the principal rights in Hutcheson's scheme of things. They are also the principal duties. He does not, like those who treat rights as a form of property, think duties arise *correlative* to rights in some negotiating give-and-take that sets up a social contract. Men have a duty to stay alive and to stay free in their thoughts and actions. Duty is simply one's right considered from another aspect.

Hutcheson was concerned with the role of virtue and moral sense in a republic. And prominent among his civic virtues was *benevolence.* To Hutcheson benevolence was not a temporary tactical mask for base selfishness; it was an abiding love of others that, as Wills puts it, "was the basic constituent of morality." The instinct for benevolence, not the abstraction of a social contract, gives rise to justice. This view, of human nature and human rights, begins with *society*, not with an atomized individual. Right arises from—and is legitimately exercised only to the extent that it promotes—the public good. It does not arise from self-interest or the individual's pursuit of advantage. This is interdependence exemplified. It is a view that in today's politics would be called "socialistic," "collectivist," "un-American." But, as Wills asserts so provocatively, it was the view of Thomas Jefferson.

It was also, of course, the view of Confucius.

> Yen Yuan asked about benevolence. The Master said, "To return to the observance of the rites through overcoming the self constitutes benevolence." (Book XII.1)

This is what excites me about China's rise and the public emergence of Chinese Americans: it will give all Americans occasion to revisit our assumptions about who we are. A time is approaching when we will be able to lay the Declaration of Independence atop *The Analects* and end up with a revelation of interdependence. Hutcheson placed a burden on his intellectual heir Jefferson, who passed that burden on to *his* intellectual heirs, including you and me, to live a certain way: as if we were citizens of a republic. *Duty is simply one's right considered from another aspect.* Confucius didn't say that, but he could have. I, an American, do.

> The Master said: "Time flows away like the water in the river."

The Hudson River, as seen from the bench by my father's gravesite, seems not just still and peaceful but constant and unmoving. Only the trees on either bank seem to change from season to season, year upon year. But that constancy is a mirage. Rivers seethe with change, with unseen turbulence and clashes of currents.

In China the Yellow River is the artery of all civilization. But rivers change course. Sometimes, as with the Three Gorges Dam on the Yangtze River, the course is changed by humans. More often, the course just changes because that is what complex systems do. In the 1940s a federal geologist made a stunning map titled "The Mississippi River Meander Belt." He had tracked, over thousands of square miles, the river's discernible course changes across more than two centuries. It's a time-lapse, color-coded transparency that shows on a single sheet all the directions in which the river has bent and cut itself off and redirected itself and straightened. The brick red river is from 1820. The light green river is from 1880. Pale blue is 1765. Uncolored is the river at the time of the mapping. The little C-shaped footprint is a tributary that was stranded. So it is with the currents of cultural norms. Quietly, America is becoming more other-directed, more mindful of mutuality. Loudly, China is becoming more selfish, more short-term, less filial, and more self-seeking. These are not fundamental shifts in the direction of the river—ours is still a culture of individuals that holds rights above and separate from responsibilities; theirs is still a culture of collectives and of duties. But in each case the river is bending, more than a bit. To walk the marshy alluvial plains and to kick up dust in the dried-up old channels, to consider a father's memory and chart the course of ghost rivers, to extrapolate rivers yet unseen: this, now, is what I am to do.

Mr. Robinson

When my mother arrived in the United States, she was twenty-one. She arrived alone, with a small bag of clothes and almost no money. The port at Baltimore, where her cargo ship pulled in, was bewildering, the chatter undecipherable. By her own wits and determination she got herself work and was soon able to go to college. But here's another side of this familiar story: my mother was already a graduate of Taiwan University, where her father had taught European history, and she already had a passable command of English. She had no money because at a port call in Tokyo she'd bought an expensive camera on the notion that she might sell it in America for a profit. She arrived alone but was met by former students of her father, who took her in while she looked for work. In every job she had, someone guided her and made her transition more humane. In one of her first jobs in the United States she was a file clerk for Chock Full o' Nuts, the Manhattan-based coffee company. She was shy and kept to herself, but most days she would bump into a kindly, older black executive named Mr. Robinson. He and his secretary made sure she was treated right. They entrusted her with important jobs like passing out each week's paychecks. Mr. Robinson always had a nice word for her in the elevator. Only many years later did she learn Mr. Robinson was an ex-ballplayer whose first name was Jackie.

So which is it? Lonely, scared, young woman immigrant, destined for the margins? Or proud new American, touched by a mythic hero, destined to claim this country as her own? Arrival stories can be told many ways.

CHAPTER 2

Mother Tongue

1.

In his book *An Anatomy of Chinese*, the scholar Perry Link observes that during the Cultural Revolution, when Mao Zedong urged his country to sweep out the old ways of doing things, the Red Guards went forth chanting slogans in the ancient Chinese poetic rhythm of *qiyan*, a seven-beat pattern. "*Ling hun shen chu, gan ge ming!*" "Make revolution in the depths of your soul!" Even Mao's name for the despised old ways—the "four olds" of customs, culture, habits, ideas—followed the venerable Chinese tradition of enumerating things to give their sum an aura of authority. This irony too was lost on Mao and his followers. It persists. In today's *new* new China, many of the catchiest commercial taglines are composed in *qiyan*'s seven beats. "*Shi ke chang xiang Mai Dang Lao!*" "Always keep McDonald's on your mind!"

The first books I can remember reading—in any language—are preschool Chinese books. Booklets, really, sixteen pages each. Simple stories in three or four vertical lines, about balls and trees and tigers. They had brightly colored folk-art drawings. The Chinese characters were neatly printed, with smaller pronunciation symbols sitting to the right of each character.

But even if those are the first readings I can recall, I surely had read something else before them. At some point my mother taught me the *bopomofo* system, the phonetic alphabet of every sound in Mandarin that accounted for those little pronunciation symbols. Each symbol was like a piece of a broken Chinese character, a fragment of DNA, or a shard of oracle bone inscription. Each symbol represented one sound. The first four sounds were *bo*, *po*, *mo*, and *fo*—hence the name of the system. There were thirty-seven sounds, to be memorized in order and repeated in a four-beat rhythm: *bo po mo fo* / *de te ne le* / *ge ke he* [rest] / *ji qi xi* [rest] / *zhi chi shi ri* / *zi ci si* [rest], and so on.

Around the same time I must have been working something out about the English alphabet. I have a borrowed recollection—a re-recollection—of writing the letter *Q* dozens of times on a piece of paper when I was not quite one year old. Borrowed, I say, because I don't remember the act itself; I remember only being told of it by my mother many, many times, from childhood to adulthood, each telling like a new coat of lacquer applied to the original. It's part of the story she formed of me: unusual (why not just draw an *O*?), directed, a touch obsessive. I can see the sheet of paper in my mind's eye. I can see my funny *Q*s. When I tell the story nowadays I usually omit that it comes from my mother's memory.

2.

In their book *Inheriting the City: The Children of Immigrants Come of Age*, the researchers Philip Kasinitz, John Mollenkopf, Mary Waters, and Jennifer Holdaway examine the role of Chinese schools in Chinese American communities. Conclusion: these schools are "remarkably unsuccessful in teaching second generation young people to read or write Chinese." Indeed, many have given up that function altogether, choosing instead to focus on SAT test prep or the teaching of folk dance.

This, in descending order of vividness, is what I remember about Chinese school: the melancholy Sunday afternoon light slanting through the windows of an unfamiliar elementary school classroom; running down the clean, unlit hallways of that school past the artwork of kids I didn't know; snack time, when we got potato chips or popcorn in cones made of rolled-up paper; the smell of the blue mimeographed grid paper on which the teacher had written the characters we now had to copy, stroke by stroke; the year my mom taught our grade, and how her voice was louder and higher than it was at home; the unmotivated mumbling of the fifteen or twenty kids as we repeated phrases in unison; the festival at Chinese New Year, when we'd get to use the gym for games like beanbag toss; the boxes full of hot McDonald's hamburgers my dad would bring to that festival; how strangely warm I felt when we watched a Chinese movie, set in ancient times, with a beautiful young woman who spoke Mandarin precisely and softly; hoping when we got home there'd be time before dinner for my neighbor John to play catch with me; learning Chinese.

3.

The Chinese language depends far more than English on context and implication. For one thing, nouns in Chinese don't typically come with an indication of number or specificity. So, for instance, the English concepts "cat," "a cat," "the cat," and "cats" would all be covered by the Chinese word *mao*. Which of those concepts *mao* was signifying at any moment would depend on the context of the conversation. Indeed, if the context has already made the specification clear, *mao* could further signify, by context, "this cat," "that cat," "these cats," "those cats," "my cat," "your cats," "all cats," and so on. This makes speaking Chinese somewhat easier—there are fewer things to get wrong in a sentence. It makes listening much harder, though. And it makes listening to what is *not* being said indispensable.

The kitchen table of my childhood was a dark brown Ethan Allen piece. It was big enough to seat the four of us—my parents and my sister and me—comfortably. It was small enough that we didn't ever have to ask anybody to pass any platters (and anyway, since my parents didn't know to teach us such American customs, we never did).

Probably a good two-thirds of my Chinese I learned at that table. I can't say I learned by listening, because I wasn't listening per se. I was just there. Mom and Dad spoke mainly to each other, and mainly in Chinese. I wasn't tuning in to the substance of their conversation, which usually had to do with my father's work at IBM, much less to the structure and syntax of it. Yet if you'd interrupted them at any point and asked me to say what they'd been discussing, I could've given a passable synopsis—in English. Their conversational Chinese simply washed over me and seeped in. I didn't consciously try to decode it any more than I consciously tried to chew the beef and broccoli before me.

One summer vacation, at that same table, my mother tried to teach Chinese to me and two other kids. This distorted my normal life in subtle, uncomfortable ways. I was at home with my mother, yes. But my mother was not behaving the way she normally did at home. There were two strangers—they were brothers, I think—in my kitchen. Each of us sat in one of the four chairs, my mother in her usual seat. When the other kids essentially stopped trying and were as disrespectful as nice Chinese kids could get, I was torn. I didn't like that they were making my mother feel impotent, but I didn't want to get in the way of their getting in the way of the lesson. I stayed silent, watching her closely. She gave up the experiment after a few lessons.

4.

Chinese is verb-heavy and noun-light compared to English. In English there is a tendency to "noun-ify" processes and actions and turn them into entities with minds of their own. Thus we get in English "ontological metaphors" like "My fear of conversation is making my mother embarrassed," in which the fear is, metaphorically, doing something. Such a metaphor, translated literally into Chinese, would result in "an awkward sentence that clearly smacks of borrowing from a Western language," as Perry Link puts it. In Chinese, fear is something one does, more than a thing with habits and interests of its own. The truly Chinese way to express the thought translates thus: "I so fear conversation that my mother can't take it."

When I was a kid, there were always two or three minutes I would dread on Chinese New Year or on my grandmothers' birthdays. My mother or father, after having been on the phone for a while with Po Po or Nai Nai to wish them well and catch up in general, would then hand me the phone to say a word of greeting. I would begin with a cheerful "*Xin Nian Kuai Le!*"

But then my grandmother would want to *converse*. I understood their questions well enough. The trouble began when I replied. While my pronunciation was good and my vocabulary sufficient, I didn't have intuitive command of the "right" way to put sentences together. As I spoke, I could tell something was just slightly off. The problem, I realize now, was that I was speaking Chinese as if it were English. That is, I'd take a sentence like "Today I told her that I will go with you" and translate it word-for-word into Chinese, when in Chinese the right way to say it would literally be, "I today tell her we together go." I used too many prepositions, making explicit all the things that in Chinese remain tacit. By the time these short encounters were over, my palms would be damp. As I sighed with relief and went back to the family room, I could hear my mom laughingly deflect my grandmother's polite praise and joke about how unfluent I truly was.

5.

Before the Berkeley cognitive linguist George Lakoff became well known for his book *Don't Think of An Elephant*, which instructed progressives how to win the game of conceptual framing in politics, he was already well known to word nerds like me for a 1980 book he and Mark Johnson wrote called *Metaphors We Live By*. This book laid bare the way that all language is made out of chunks of metaphor, as we bootstrap from one metaphorical concept to another (laying bare, making, chunks, bootstraps). It cataloged dozens of tropes of metaphor—"argument as war," "excellence as height," "emotion as volume"—and was a revelation.

But not every pattern of metaphor that Lakoff and Johnson described for English holds true in Chinese. For instance, because Chinese tends to dispense with words like "with," the

English metaphor "instrument as companion"—that is, our use of "with" to signify instrumentality, as in "I cut this apple with a knife"—is nonsensical in Chinese. In Chinese it's just, "I use knife cut this apple." The use of metaphor in general is one of the key ways the languages differ. American English more frequently uses metaphors of selling and sports competitions, whereas Chinese uses metaphors of cooking, eating, and family. In *Metaphor, Culture, and Worldview,* linguist Dilin Liu observes that to "call the shots" means in English what *dang jia* or "represent the household" means in Chinese: to be in control. To "get more than you bargained for" is to "not be able to finish eating" (*chi bu liao*). And the Chinese equivalent of "winner take all" is *yingzhe tong chi,* "winner eat all."

I cannot recall a single time my father or mother told me to study harder, demanded I get great grades, directed me to set my sights on Yale or Harvard, or impressed upon me the need to excel in all things. This is in part because I was a pretty self-motivated kid. But really, it just wasn't their way to be pushy or even that involved in what I was doing. They did not fit the stereotype of hyper-pragmatic, controlling Chinese parents—what today would be called "Tiger parents."

By the time I was in junior high or high school, I realized my parents were relatively "cool"—laid-back, that is. I felt fortunate, compared not just to other Chinese American kids but also, say, to my second-generation Greek friend George, whose parents could be almost comically tough on him. When my buddies came over for a sleepover or just to hang out, Mom and Dad spoke in English to us all. They could have shifted back to Chinese with me, but they chose not to, lest they put distance between my friends and me. My heart ached a bit at the gesture, and again, when Dad would cheerfully bring out a tray of cookies and chips and soda for us. "Have snacks!"

At the same time, I also cannot recall a single time either my father or my mother said to me, "Good job" or "We're proud of you" or "Congratulations." They didn't cheer me at sports events or praise me after a recital. I am not sure they ever came to a track meet or a wrestling match. I note this without an iota of self-pity or resentment. It would have been as unnecessary as their saying, "Your name is Eric." There was an unstated sense that when you're capable of doing well—by talent and/or circumstance—you should simply do well. What I do recall were little darts of disdain they aimed at people who were stupid or lazy or—the most judgmental label a person could ever get—*meiyouyong*, "without use," "useless." Here was not just moral opprobrium but also an implied whiff of the competitiveness that was otherwise absent from their relaxed style of parenting. The message I absorbed, wordlessly, was that life is a competition to be the most useful.

6.

Among the most prevalent metaphors in Chinese, observes Dilin Liu, are acting and singing metaphors that derive from Beijing opera. To humor someone halfheartedly is to *fu yan*, or "perform skin-deep." To oppose someone is to *chang fan diao*, or "sing a contrary tune." When there's nothing left to be done, it's *mei xi*, or "no play."

Richard Rodriguez wrote a generation ago about the gap between the intimacy of private language and the necessity of public language. For him and his immigrant Mexican parents, Spanish was the private tongue that had to be shed in order for him to assimilate, via English, into public life. Today this seems needlessly binary—not only because the bilingualism he opined against in the 1980s didn't end up fracturing America irreparably, but also, more basically, because loss and gain rarely occur in a one-for-one trade. They sit side by side, amid the ambiguities of our actual lives.

There's a third language, which I call "public private": the language of home when used outside the home. I heard lots of public private Chinese at parties my parents hosted for their fellow immigrants from Taiwan, at gatherings of my uncles and aunts, or at picnics or festivals with the Chinese community. In the company of friends and relatives—of peers—my mother and father spoke a kind of Chinese that was a touch more stagy, more playfully exaggerated or rhetorical than home speech. They weren't outright acting; they just injected a dose of winking theatricality—*Oh,* now *you agree with me! How could* I *do that?*—with the affect of public speech. It was all the more private, more inside, for the pretense.

7.

One of the great debates in linguistics centers on the Sapir-Whorf Hypothesis. The idea, developed by Edward Sapir and Benjamin Whorf and popularized in the 1950s, posits that the structure of a language limits and even determines how speakers of that language think. So if a language has many words for X, then native speakers of that language will see the world disproportionately in terms of X. (Thus the well-known myth that Eskimos have a hundred different words for snow.)

Modern-day critics, like cognitive scientist Steven Pinker, have mocked the hypothesis as circular reasoning and reject its so-called linguistic determinism. Like Noam Chomsky before him, Pinker asserts that there is a universal human wiring for thought that *precedes* language or culture and is wholly independent of both: we all see many different kinds of snow, gray and slushy or pure and hard or wispy and fleeting; it's just a matter of how we describe it. The debate over Sapir-Whorf has been heated, even polemical, in the way of academic debates, with no decisive evidence on either side.

From a lay perspective, it seems reality lies between the two positions—indeed, must be a combination of them. You don't have to subscribe to the notion that culture wholly determines cognition (even Whorf didn't go that far) to recognize that the names people give things influence how they see things. (See, for instance, "pro-life" versus "anti-choice.") You can imagine that humans at birth share a universal wiring for what Pinker calls "mentalese," a prelanguage mode of making sense of the world, while still acknowledging that once born a universal human is raised in a particular place, time, and cultural context—and that the practices of that culture, not least its language, can indeed shape how the baby grows up thinking. From this position, it's possible to say that Chinese people aren't *inherently*—that is, genetically and biologically—predisposed to emphasize relationships and context more than Europeans; but that when Chinese people are raised in a typically Chinese cultural environment, speaking and hearing Chinese, they do take on such values, and when they aren't, they don't.

That space of possibility is what the Michigan psychologist Richard Nisbett has explored. His work examines *How Asians and Westerners Think Differently . . . and Why*, the subtitle of his 2003 book *The Geography of Thought*. Challenges pop up immediately, of course. What, exactly, is an "Asian" or a "Westerner"? Is there truly anything meaningful to be learned about such broad, even essentializing, comparisons? But read his research more closely, and interesting patterns emerge. Nisbett and his colleagues gave word triplets (panda, monkey, banana) to Chinese college students in China and European American college students in the United States. The students were asked to say which two in each set were most closely related. The Chinese students tended to create clusters based on relationship (monkey, banana), whereas the white American students created clusters based on taxonomical category (panda, monkey).

Nisbett then used a finer-toothed comb. He ran the test with ethnic Chinese students who were bilingual. Some, from China and Taiwan, were native Chinese speakers who had learned English later in life. Some, from Hong Kong and Singapore, had learned English relatively early. It turns out the second group, with earlier and more exposure to English, was more likely to gravitate toward taxonomy groupings than the first group—but that when compared with white American students, the second group was more likely to gravitate toward *relationship* groupings. It turns out there is a continuum of Whorfian influence, an implied principle of relativity: how Chinese you seem in thought and habit depends in part on whom you're next to. Which, for this native speaker of English exposed to Chinese early on, raised a question: Is "Chinese American" a relationship or a category?

When we were children, most of my cousins could speak Chinese much more fluently than I did. This was discomfiting. Within my adolescent heart were two warring impulses. Impulse 1: I wanted to fit in with my own relatives and avoid the pitying glance of an aunt or uncle as I answered their Chinese questions in English. Impulse 2: I wanted to dampen this shame with the thought that none of my cousins could match me for integration into the American mainstream. Which may have been true. But now I wonder: Does claiming Americanness truly compensate for losing Chineseness?

8.

From the Greeks to the American pragmatists, Western philosophers have pondered the meaning of ideas like "the good." But as we learn in Perry Link's *An Anatomy of Chinese*, it's cumbersome to create a Chinese phrase that conveys "the good"—or, for that matter, any concept that makes an adjective a noun, including most English words that end with "ness." Happiness. Bigness. Whiteness. This "nessness," as I call it, is a condition that Chinese semantics and syntax simply do not contemplate. "There is the whiteness of the horse or the whiteness of the snow in ancient Chinese philosophy," writes Nisbett, "but not whiteness as an abstract, detachable concept that can be applied to almost anything."

If to be *meiyouyong*—"useless"—was a sin during my youth, to *dong shi* was divine. *Dong shi*: "to understand things." What things, specifically? How to be thoughtful. How to be polite. How to have discretion. How not to make others look or feel bad. How to be appropriate. This was a matter of inductive learning. There was no guidebook. It was a matter, too, of negative reinforcement. I learned via scoldings. *Ni tai bu dong shi!* "You are *so* not thoughtful/polite/discreet/attuned/appropriate!" My crime might have been asking Dad to take me to the mall when he was clearly tired after dialysis. Or saying something that inadvertently offended a guest. Or standing by dumbly as someone else offered to clear the table. I noticed that most often it was other, more socially mature Chinese kids my age whom my parents praised as *dong shi.* Rarely did a white friend, no matter how polite, earn the designation.

9.

In Chinese, the placement of a single word can collapse time. Verbs are typically put into past tense when followed by the article *le.* But if you insert the word *kuai*, which means "fast" or "quick," ahead of the verb that's followed by *le,* then the sentence no longer signifies completed action; it now signifies impending action. Thus:

Wo chi.	I eat.
Wo chi le.	I ate/have eaten.
Wo kuai chi le.	I'm just about to eat.

Wo xue.	I learn.
Wo xue le.	I learned/have learned.
Wo kuai xue le.	I'm just about to learn.

Put a hint of speed in front of the past to signal that change is imminent.

When I got to college, I decided to take Level 1 Chinese. The idea was to go back to the beginning and retrace the steps that had brought me to a child's level of patchwork proficiency. Of course, I had an advantage over classmates who'd never heard, much less tried to say, the four tones of Mandarin. But this advantage of exposure actually made things harder for me at first, in the way that someone who has been an amateur, untrained athlete can suddenly lose his ability when under proper coaching he's forced to spell out his tacit knowledge, pay explicit attention to movements, and unlearn bad habits.

After an initial phase of self-consciousness, though, I found it enormously satisfying to learn precisely why certain rhythms and sentence constructions had always felt "right" and certain others just hadn't. There was a hidden logic behind it all. My textbooks spelled it out at a level of detail that might have been mind-numbing to some—there were whole chapters on when to use *le* and for which of many purposes—but for me was thrilling. For the first time, I heard clearly what my relatives had been saying—that is, I understood the rules that governed their speech, rules I'd noticed but hadn't systematized and couldn't replicate in my own speech. Now I could. I could converse with my grandmothers, no sheepish apology required. In certain moments, I could muster or at least mimic some of the mock-stagy confidence of the joshing between my father and his friends. Even though my vocabulary remained limited, I started speaking Chinese *as if* I were fluent—as if I'd gone back in time and given myself years of fluency.

Then, after doing four semesters and completing Level 2, I stopped. I felt I had enough to get by. I could do everyday conversation now. I wasn't interested in being able to read the Chinese newspaper or talk politics or history in Chinese. I had become interested in talking politics and history in *English*. Diplomacy, strategy, European great power rivalries, military history, American political history: this is what I wanted to fill my credit hours and my brain with. So I did. That brief moment, when I could glimpse being more than passable at Chinese, passed.

10.

From *Spoken Standard Chinese*, volume 1, by Parker Po-Fei Huang and Hugh M. Stimson:

> 12.9 *The experiential verbal suffix -guo*. This suffix indicates that the actions of the verb to which it is suffixed happened at least once in the past. It differs from the past tense verbal suffix *guo (–guo)* in always carrying the neutral tone and in never occurring with the sentence particle *le* that means "action completed in the past." . . .

ni dao Ouzhou 'quguo meiyou?	Have you ever been to Europe?
wo mei quguo.	No, I haven't.
ni chiguo Zhongguo fan ma?	Have you ever eaten Chinese food?
wo chiguo. Women chang chi Zhongguo fan.	Yes, I have. We often eat Chinese food.

In short: the same suffix *guo* (literally, "pass by") can be used in two subtly different contexts, one to signify something that happened, the other to signify an experience that's been had. How wide is this gap between "It happened" and "I have had this experience"?

One of my great regrets is that my father never knew I was a speechwriter for an American president. I think he would have felt a specific kind of pride. He wouldn't have been boastful; that wasn't his way. He would have been gratified as a fellow wordsmith. Though Chao-hua Liu was never officially in the word business, he was nonetheless a master. His ear—his instinct for killer ways to make a point, both logically and musically—was nearly as good in English as it was in Chinese. He would have been proud that my command of my native language had given me this opportunity. He would also have discerned, I like to think, how a lifetime of being steeped in my second language—a tongue of poetic conventions, implied meanings, freighted terseness—had shaped my instrument.

By far the most consequential speeches I wrote for President Clinton were for the 1994 commemoration of the fiftieth anniversary of D-Day and the Allied invasion of Normandy. Here was a Gen X son of Chinese immigrants crafting words for the first baby boomer president and a son of the South, as he thanked the GI generation and the father he never knew. At his remarks at the American military cemetery at Colleville-sur-Mer, facing rows of aged veterans of the Longest Day, President Clinton spoke for seven minutes. I mouthed the words as they came out of his mouth. And when I saw those tough old men in the front row quaver as they tried but failed to stem the tide of tears, I too began to cry. Like a child.

> Oh, they may walk with a little less spring in their step, and their ranks are growing thinner. But let us never forget: When they were young, these men saved the world. . . .
>
> For just as freedom has a price, it also has a purpose, and its name is progress. . . .
>
> Our parents did that and more; we must do nothing less. They struggled in war so that we might strive in peace.

Lines like these did not follow the five- or seven-beat cadence of *wuyan* or *qiyan*. They were crafted in the idiom of this country, this language. They borrowed from the plain-speaking testimony of GIs, the classical parallelism and antitheticality of a Lincoln or a Kennedy, the idealistic folksiness of a Reagan. These were not Chinese rhythms. But what I had learned from Chinese was that rhythm itself has meaning—that rhythm *is* meaning, because a particular pattern of beats can evoke a particular place and time. What I had learned from Chinese was that when words leave the tongue just so, we can, if but for a moment, claim another's memory as our own.

A Guide to Punctuation

Chinese-American

This is the standard grammatical form for describing an American of Chinese ethnicity. But that hyphen vexes me: it implies an interaction rather than a person. As in: "Chinese-American cooperation," or "Chinese-American conflict," or "Chinese-American commerce." I am not merely an adjectival description of a transaction. I am a noun. I am a person.

Chinese/American

I've always thought the slash would be a useful way for many first-generation immigrants to signify their state of mind: more harshly divided than the hyphenated form—interrupted, even. The slash signifies the bifurcated life of the person born and raised in one land who then births and raises children in another. It plays, when spoken, not as a single phrase but as two, separated by staccato silence: Chinese (slight pause). American (sigh).

Chinese, American

Here's a way to list identities as if on an application form ("Please indicate national cultures in which you are fluent or proficient"). This is for the cosmopolitan who truly does live in both countries and cultures (or more than two), and for whom identity feels like a wholly elective affair, a menu from which to choose and within which to delineate a sequence, a considered and implicit priority. You could imagine this being just the start of a list (Chinese, American, Jamaican, Dutch, Honduran . . .).

Chinese (American)

This seems to be the right way to punctuate the person whose Americanness is an afterthought—either because she lives in a Chinatown enclave that only in its barely visible infrastructure is American and is otherwise saturated in Chineseness, or because she is so secure in her ability to navigate mainstream America that she can wear Chineseness like a jade adornment.

(Chinese) American

Inversely, this ought to be how very assimilated people are identified. Only passingly Chinese, trying hard to pass for not-at-all Chinese.

$\frac{\text{Chinese}}{\text{American}}$

A mathematical notation worth pondering. Chineseness is the numerator, the thing ever to be divided, diluted; Americanness, the denominator, the base against which the other thing is compared, pressed, and brought down to size. The older I get, the more I realize this notation captures the intergenerational experience—the rate of change, as they say in calculus. Or decay.

Chinese American

This form of nonpunctuated punctuation is powerful, a thing of beauty. It consists of a modifier and the modified. That's it. "American" is the noun, preceded by the adjective depicting what kind, what style, what flavor, what shape of American: "Chinese." No qualifications, provisos, footnotes, ambiguities. The only thing between the two halves is a tiny bit of white space.

CHAPTER 3

Overseas Chinese

Di·as·po·ra *n.* A dispersion of an originally homogeneous entity, such as a language or culture.

> Diaspora is dispersion. From the Greek *diaspeiro*: "I scatter."
> Diaspora is the scattering about of seeds.
> Diaspora, says the Bible, is exile.

IT'S REMARKABLE, WHEN YOU THINK ABOUT IT. A TINY nation of islands populated by a ragtag amalgam of Nordic, Germanic, Frankish, and Celtic people ends up casting its hybrid seed all over the planet. On every continent and virtually every country you can find lineal descendants of this British tribe. And their behavior is truly tribal. Whether in Nairobi or Delhi or Hong Kong or Kuala Lumpur or Panama City, these British keep to themselves, speak their native tongue, socialize with and marry each other, maintain a distinctness that is both cultural and genetic and so strong that it becomes hard to distinguish between mores and genes. Almost everywhere they are to be found, these Britishers are in positions of outsize power, wealth, and influence. They are overachievers. They have their own interlocking networks for doing business and influencing politics. They are often the object of resentment and conspiracy theories in the non-British ethnic majorities that surround them. But they have proven as resilient as the cockroach, surviving the centuries and adapting to varied terrains of politics, economics, and climate. This is the remarkable story of the Overseas British.

Actually, it's not. Or, rather, it's not the way we are used to hearing the story of those whose descendants hail from Britannia. This narrative, in this context, strikes us as both foreign and familiar. It's foreign because we simply don't talk about the British and their progeny this way. Whether as Anglo-Saxons or as WASPs or merely as whites, they are just there, the norm, the background against which other groups, particularly in America, have historically been noticed and measured. But it's familiar because this story—of a clannish tribe that is dispersed around the world yet assiduously maintains its essential distinctiveness, refusing to assimilate and on some level unassimilable, its members in diaspora using secret methods to insinuate themselves into host societies and attach leechlike to the vessels of lucre and influence—this is a story we have indeed heard before.

We've heard it told of the Jews, and still do, though it is generally not polite anymore to say it.

We've heard it told of the Chinese, and still do. Politeness has little to do with it.

Who ever says "the British in America"? The British by now are just the base stock of the American soup, their genes intermingled and their names (Williams, Johnson, Adams) carried by descendants white and black. The Irish, as others have described, long ago became white. But "the Chinese in America" still sounds somewhat appropriate, even *current*—that is, it doesn't have quite the anachronistic, even absurd ring of "the British in America"—because Chinese people in America still have a high enough FQ (foreignness quotient) to prompt a millisecond flicker of doubt in the eyes and hearts of our compatriots. Flash my visage across a screen, and then ask your subject to think of a country. If he is an American, his first reflexive association is still China. Another millisecond later, when he hears my standard American English, when he sees my facial muscles move with an American openness or sense of irony, when he hears me laugh with a wide open mouth, when he notices countless other cues of comportment, he will make that instant adjustment and tell himself, "Oh—American."

China's arrival as a great power is the furthest-reaching geopolitical narrative of our time, more significant than wars on terror and Arab uprisings, more economically consequential than financial collapse and near-Depression. But it's already been so assimilated as background knowledge, as a veritable law of nature, that it hardly occurs to us to imagine in detail the reach of the coordinated Chinese push for global domination. From time to time, though, a reminder of that coordination and intention arrives with sobering force. A simple world map in the *New York Times* accompanying a 2013 essay called "China's Economic Empire" shows the places all around the planet, from Congo to Costa Rica, from Greenland to Siberia to Sudan to Uzbekistan, where Chinese foreign direct investment, Chinese laborers, joint ventures with Chinese state-owned enterprises, Chinese energy pipelines, Chinese extraction of iron ore and other commodities, Chinese pressure to force the relaxation of local rules on wages and standards, Chinese controlling interests in other nations' iconic companies like Volvo and Smithfield Farms and Club Med, Chinese ownership of whole ports in Greece and other choke points of global commerce all add up to one thing: a plan to take over the world commercially, a push that the essay calls by turns "unstoppable" and "disturbing," "aggressive" and "rapacious."

In his best-selling book *When the Chinese Rule the World*, the English political commentator Martin Jacques writes of the power of the "Overseas Chinese," the worldwide diaspora of Chinese who have become something of an advance force—scouts, pioneers, *infiltrators*—for China's imperial economic ambitions. During the run-up to the 2008 Beijing Olympics, he writes, in some nations thousands and sometimes tens of thousands of Overseas Chinese organized to demonstrate in support of the Games (and to outshout critics of China's Tibet policies). In Ho Chi Minh City, in Canberra and Nagano and other capitals, these prideful, increasingly vocal people of Chinese descent are just a small part of a vast forty-million-strong network of people who, according to this idea of the Overseas Chinese, are Chinese first and Chinese last.

This idea long predates the contemporary era of Chinese might. Indeed, its origins lie in periods of Chinese weakness across the centuries. When the Qing Dynasty began to falter in the nineteenth century, its control of the country eroded by warlords within and imperialists from abroad, great waves of poor, unskilled Chinese dispersed to other lands. All across Southeast Asia, but also across Latin America and Europe and Africa, countless Chinese sojourned and settled. It is not surprising to learn there are over 9 million Chinese in Thailand or nearly 7 million in Malaysia. It is a bit more surprising to learn there are 600,000 Chinese in France, over 300,000 in South Africa, and 1.1 million in Peru.

In most of the nations where migrant Chinese settled, their communities started out isolated and spurned and had to make a virtue of necessity. They maintained social and cultural coherence, creating closed networks and associations for mutual aid and investment. Most were coolie laborers, living in brutal conditions, though in many places they eventually became merchants and middlemen, brokers and bargainers. Some became prosperous; all were assumed to be part of a vast ethnic conspiracy, and they provoked resentment for their clannish ways, their alien tongue, their insider dealings and secret code for success.

This, of course, is not just a Chinese story. So-called middleman minorities, like Jews throughout Europe and Indians in East Africa, have often achieved vastly outsized clout. But the Chinese diaspora is in a league of its own for scale, reach, duration, and influence. In the Philippines, for instance, the Chinese constitute 1 percent of the population but control 60 percent of the wealth. Long before Amy Chua became the Tiger Mother, she wrote a book called *World on Fire* predicting that backlashes against such "market-dominant minorities" would result in waves of ethnic political conflict and violence. Picture it: tens of millions of Overseas Chinese as the kindling for transcontinental conflagration. A world on fire.

There are nearly four million people of Chinese ancestry in the United States, making this "the largest overseas Chinese community in North America and the fourth-largest in the Chinese diaspora," says Wikipedia in its entry on Chinese Americans. I don't doubt the accuracy of the statistics. I do note, however, the usage here of "overseas Chinese." The implication persists that Chinese Americans are merely the local branch of some Global League of Chinese. One reason why is that some Chinese Americans and many Chinese nationals living here indeed see themselves this way. But the main reason is that no country this century will pose a greater competitive challenge to the United States than China.

The treatment of Chinese Americans has always depended in great measure on the strength or weakness of China. In the nineteenth and early twentieth century, when China was at its weakest, the treatment was at its worst. We are now in the midst of an experiment: What happens when China is at its strongest?

The more powerful China becomes, the more Chinese Americans are perceived as vessels of such power. The more discomfitingly assertive China is, the more Chinese Americans are seen as discomfitingly assertive in their dealings. The more underhanded, the more deceptive, the more inscrutably treacherous China's moves appear, the more Chinese Americans are assumed to be all these things.

China's magnetic force seems so powerful now that it can pry loose from American society veins of precious talent, no matter how deeply embedded, and pull them straight back across the sea. In some tellings, we Chinese Americans are those veins of ore. Or maybe it's a different story of magnetism. Maybe we Chinese Americans are loose iron filings lying around in the open hodgepodge tray of America, just waiting for that day when—*zing!*—the great magnet will approach and we can fly up from the tray and (re)attach ourselves to the core from whence we came.

Consider this, from the *New York Times*, page 1, column 1, June 6, 2013. Headline: "China Seen in Push to Gain Technology Insights." Dateline: Shenzhen, China, where a government research institute is financing all manner of high-tech innovation. Storyline: Prosecutors in the US have charged three "Chinese scientists" at the New York University School of Medicine with accepting bribes to funnel research findings and other secrets to the Shenzhen institute.

Midway through the article there is a quote from Frank Wu, a legal scholar and dean of Hastings College of Law, warning against drawing overbroad conclusions about the activities of people of Chinese ancestry in America. The article then goes on for many paragraphs, each amplifying a sense of vague unease, and inviting the reader to draw, well, overbroad conclusions. Only at the end does the article return to the actual case of the three accused Chinese scientists at the NYU School of Medicine.

Here is a question it does not explore: Are those "three Chinese scientists" Chinese or American? Here is another question it does not explore: Shouldn't it matter?

American-born Chinese.

It's the title of an acclaimed popular graphic novel by Gene Yuen that chronicles the awkward suburban adolescence of a son of Chinese immigrants. It is also the title many such children are given by their Chinese immigrant parents. "ABC" is the shorthand form, and it's kind of a putdown, said with gentle derision or outright dismay. "You ABCs think if you know how to order dim sum you Chinese." Or "You ABCs can't handle spicy food." Or "You ABCs think you can just get whatever you want without working for it." I can hear many Chinese parents, not just mine, addressing us kids as "you ABCs," with exactly the kind of overgeneralizing dismissiveness that offends, say, African Americans when they're addressed by whites as "you people."

The idea is that because we were born in America we can't quite hack it as Chinese. We don't have the chops(ticks). We know too little about Chinese culture. We speak too little of the language too poorly. We take for granted all the little luxuries of this affluent, materialistic society. We're soft. We're a watered-down imitation of the real thing, with a diluted work ethic, a diluted appreciation for tradition. Nothing about being "American-born" is meant to be a compliment.

Yet the very wording "American-born Chinese" implies that, in spite of the corrupting effects of my American environs, I am, at bottom, Chinese. To be called "ABC" by your parents is to hear both their grief that you are changing and their belief that you won't. I do not recall ever hearing someone of my parents' generation address their kids as Chinese American, much less simply as American. We were American-born, not American.

It takes no small amount of wishful thinking to imagine second-generation people like me, people who grew up in the American mediasphere and civic square, as essentially Chinese. What makes that clear is being viewed from the vantage of our supposed "co-ethnics"—the Chinese in China. If I am truly simply an Overseas Chinese, an American-born Chinese, then I should be able, on short notice, to shuck off the costume of my Americanness, make a crossing back to my homeland, and be united again with my blood brethren.

Indeed, never in history have so many Overseas Chinese, particularly from America, wished to go back to China. There are hundreds of thousands of Chinese-born undergraduate and graduate students who now comprise the largest foreign student population in the United States; most intend to return after their studies. Then there are immigrants from China who had perhaps intended to settle in America but now look for opportunities to do business in China. And last there are the children and grandchildren of those immigrants, born and raised in the United States but now similarly drawn to go "back home" in search of opportunity. The opportunity is there. Many ABCs are getting rich today, starting their own ventures in China or working for big American companies that need the smoothing, intermediary presence of bilingual Chinese Americans.

But make no mistake. When we are in China, we ABCs are reminded many ways a day that we are not truly Chinese. We may look Chinese. But cab drivers and street vendors can size us up instantly and address us a bit dismissively with tiny shards of broken English. This is microevidence of a tectonic shift in attitude. It wasn't long ago that a Chinese American touring or working in China was treated by the average Chinese with a touch of deference, not as a less-than but as a more-than. As Chinese-plus. That has changed.

When Gary Locke was governor of Washington, his 1997 "homecoming" to his family's ancestral village, Jilong, was a glorious occasion. His grandfather had immigrated to America in the 1890s, finding work as a houseboy in Olympia, Washington, less than a mile away from the governor's mansion that Locke would come to call home. The Chinese media treated Locke like a celebrity, following him at every stop and showering him with adoration. They played up his family roots and the fact that Washington, home of Boeing and Microsoft, has strong trading ties to China.

Then in 2011 he was named US ambassador to China. At first the reception was similarly adulatory. Early reports marveled at how humble and down-to-earth Locke was. A photo of him at an airport Starbucks, waiting in line to get his own coffee and carrying his own bags, became a viral sensation in China. It turned out, though, that the sensation was less about love of Locke per se than it was an indirect criticism of the Audi-chauffeured princelings and party powerbrokers who rule China today. Once Locke settled into his job—which, after all, was not to please Chinese people but to represent the interests of the United States—he on occasion became the object of orchestrated scorn. Special scorn, for he was not just American but Chinese American. Locke's predecessor, the Mormon, Mandarin-speaking Jon Huntsman, had also been criticized by Chinese citizens. But now nationalist mobs of those citizens pelted Locke's car during anti-Japanese (and implicitly anti-American) riots. They pointed out that Locke is unable to speak Chinese. They excoriated him in online forums for being a fake, a lapdog, and, odd as it may seem, a traitor to his race.

But what he was, was simply this: an American, overseas.

When Locke was ten, his parents had brought him from Seattle's Beacon Hill neighborhood to Hong Kong. The plan was to leave him with his grandmother and to immerse him for a year in Chinese schools and Chinese culture. Locke hated it. He was mocked by school kids for not being able to speak Chinese. He missed his home, his Boy Scout troop, his parents. After only a few months, they relented and brought him back. Brought him home. It turns out—and Gary Locke, one-time hero of the diaspora, is proof of this—that there is no such thing, really, as an ABC. To be American-born is inherently, inescapably to become something other than pure Chinese. It is, indeed, to highlight that there may never have been such a thing as pure Chinese. Purity of Chineseness is a fiction imagined and nurtured by those who migrated and by those they left behind to mask a sense of loss, to mark the distance traveled, to reckon with the reality that any hope for purity ended, on some level, the moment they who set sail set sail.

What is a seed, Dearly Beloved? Is a fish not a seed? May we not open the fish to find the sea? Do the birds know what they carry?

—Li-Young Lee, *The Winged Seed*

There are many dialects of spoken Chinese, from Shanghainese to Toishanese to Mandarin. Sometimes the aural distance between them is like the distance between Mississippi English and Boston English. In other cases it is the distance between English and Greek. But there is only one written Chinese language, used by the speakers of every tongue generically called "Chinese." It is the constant, the glue that binds all these speakers of all these different dialects from all these separate provinces that might otherwise begin to think of themselves as separate nations.

Many Americans know that written Chinese characters are ideographs, derived from primitive symbols. Most do not know, however, that written Chinese comes in two formats, *fantizi* and *jiantizi*, complex and simplified. So-called complex Chinese characters are what was traditionally written, read, and taught in China for thousands of years. Simplified characters were implemented by the Communists in the 1950s and 1960s in response to the mass illiteracy of the nation's peasantry. It was a great feat of linguistic engineering. Simplified characters dramatically reduce the number of strokes in each character and make reading and writing far easier. Many lamented this "dumbing-down" of written Chinese: the subversion of the nuance, beauty, and tactile intricacy of the original characters. Indeed, in Taiwan, where the Nationalist government fled in 1949, simplified Chinese is not in use. But there is no denying that because of simplification, many millions of people over several generations have learned to read. And it is their ability to read that gives added force now to their burgeoning sense of Chineseness.

As it is with Chinese characters, so it is with Chinese *character*. There is a complex original. It is sprawling and unwieldy. Then comes a simplified version, easier to retain and transmit. But is something lost in the simplification? What is the essence of Chineseness? And does a more abstract, less detailed representation of that essence truly do it justice?

National character is both real and imagined. It is real because it is imagined and imagined because real.

The popular, simplified conception of Chinese national character (*guomingxing*) begins with the fact that China has long called itself Zhong Guo, "center nation" or, in the better-known translation, the Middle Kingdom. A presumption of greatness. Other popular notions of Chinese character hold that the Chinese are tradition-minded, thanks to Confucius and his heirs, and noninterventionist, thanks to Taoism; they cherish order because of China's long history of warlordism, chaos, and foreign rapacity; they take a long and cyclical view of life because Chinese history affords one of the longest views available of recorded human experience. They are resilient and have weathered the worst that heaven and earth can deal out.

But there are other things that people, including Chinese people, sometimes say are part of Chinese national character. For one: a suffocating conformity that leaves only a vestige of individualism, as warped and rotted as the crushed bones of bound feet. Moreover: unthinking obedience to central authority, rationalized by a pragmatic unwillingness to stick one's neck out. Sublimated pain and anxiety that come out in periodic paroxysms of mass insanity. And then something subtler, what the 1920s reformist author Lu Xun called an "Ah-Q" mentality in his famous short story. Ah-Q, a tragicomic everyman, kisses up to his social superiors but heaps scorn down on his peers and lessers. He fails in his day-to-day dealings with people but deludes himself into believing that each setback is actually an advance. He is boastful, small-minded, nitpicky, legalistic, oblivious to the reality of the world around him until a series of events carries him like a cork on a current to his execution.

Which of these notions of Chinese character is true? National character is a chimera, a quantum reality neither here nor there yet both at once. When the current president of China, Xi Jinping, ascended to power, he began to deliver speeches championing what he dubbed "the Chinese Dream." This Chinese Dream is, in the first place, a reaction. It is an answer to the fact that America has the American Dream and that an American columnist, Thomas Friedman of the *New York Times*, wrote, "China needs its own dream." Soon the state marketing machine was selling one. The Chinese Dream is deliberately vague, a blend of official slogan and unofficial buzzword, but in its broad strokes it seeks to do rhetorically what simplified Chinese characters do lexically: remove complexities, create unity. The Chinese Dream, according to the keepers of Communist Party doctrine, consists of four clean parts: Strong China, Civilized China, Harmonious China, Beautiful China.

Some reformers in China hope that "Beautiful" means a greater emphasis on environmental sustainability or that "Civilized" means more individual liberty. Others interpret

"Harmonious" to mean greater equity in the spread of prosperity. Much hope—many a dream—is invested in the meaning of these words. No one is quite sure if these beams of doctrine can actually bear this much weight, but then, it doesn't actually matter what the particulars are or whether there even are any codified particulars. The Chinese Dream is mainly about *having* a Chinese Dream and being able to announce it.

It's also a fairy tale. Or, rather, a fable. This is not to be harsh. Every nation's story of its own character—and every nation's story of *other* nations' character—begins with a moral and works backwards. That is certainly true of the tale we tell in America of our own can-do, ruggedly individualist character. What's important is to ask *why* we tell these stories and why we filter out evidence that contradicts them.

Two decades before Xi Jinping's Chinese Dream, Lee Kuan Yew, then the benevolent autocrat of Singapore, peddled a morality tale called "Asian Values." The West, he said, should not harshly judge Asians, and especially the Chinese, for their approach to human rights. Asians have their *own* values, Lee argued, that prioritize the good of the whole over the good of the individual, the need for stability over the need for freedom. And his kicker was: *they work*. Asian economic success was proof, he said, that these values were right for Asians. Never mind that the Cambridge-educated "Harry" Lee, running a former British colony, was living testimony to the universalizing power of Western values. Never mind that "Asian" was too soggy a bag for all the cultural traditions he was trying to stuff into it. The Fable of Asian Values was an elegant closed-loop justification for soft authoritarianism.

As China grew mightier in the ensuing years, Lee became one of the era's most vocal evangelists of an Overseas Chinese revival. He said that whether they lived in Canada, Australia, the United States, or Europe, ethnic Chinese should see themselves as members of a tribe. They should nurture their ethnic network. They should exploit their *guanxi*—their connections, to one another, and to their cultural motherland—to generate business and get deals done and further the cause of progress. Now countless others, East and West, have taken up this gospel of co-ethnic networking, of Confucian capitalism. The idea of *guanxi* as gold, or at least the way to find and mine gold, has yielded a secondary industry in China of cultural brokers who sell nothing more than knowledge of how to get and use *guanxi*.

It's all very convenient. But what if this same story, this same tale of indelible Chineseness that says you can take a Chinese out of China but not the China out of Chinese—what if it were to be deployed not just by China-boosters in search of profits but also by China-bashers in search of scapegoats? What if this spidery web of Chinese ethnic connection was seen not as beneficial to global capital flow and efficient exchange of goods but as a spider's web, meant to ensnare and incapacitate prey?

Much of the media coverage of China and its dealings with America can be understood more clearly if you conduct a simple thought experiment: imagine that the reports are describing not people but pathogens. Or parasites.

Chinese hackers burrowing their way into American bank accounts and into classified US military servers. The rise of Chinese "birth tourism," in which pregnant Chinese women are flown to the United States so their babies, born on American soil, can claim citizenship here and gain access to all the benefits of that status. Chinese nationals seeking placement in American corporations and research centers, waiting patiently to steal our secrets. Chinese investors using innocuous shell companies buying up distressed properties and businesses across the United States. Chinese international students paying full freight at cash-strapped state universities across the United States, thus taking up slots for deserving in-state residents.

Now, try to stop the thought experiment.

Now, look at a Chinese American.

"Chinese people have a strong feeling of comradeship toward overseas Chinese," a Japanese observer told the *New York Times* a few years ago. "Overseas Chinese have a long tradition, and they remain Chinese even after generations have passed. Japanese regard second- or third-generation overseas Japanese, even though they are of Japanese origin, as 'people from that country over there.'"

It's certainly true that the Japanese do not have a mythology of Overseas Diaspora the way the Chinese do. Indeed, they make sharp distinctions between Japanese from Japan and Japanese not from Japan, distinctions in some ways as sharp as those between Japanese and non-Japanese. Alberto Fujimori, the ethnic Japanese Peruvian who rose to the presidency of Peru and then was deposed, landing in exile in Japan, was throughout his public life named in the Japanese media using *katakana* rather than *kanji*—a form of written language that signifies foreignness rather than Japaneseness.

In the late 1980s, Japan was facing a labor shortage as its export boom began. A labor shortage in Japan is not just an economic challenge; it's a civilizational one. Japan, with its ingrained sense of racial purity, does not embrace immigration or immigrants. There have long been guest workers from other countries in Japan, but business and government leaders, uncomfortable with the idea of bringing in more Pakistanis or Bangladeshis, came up with a new idea in 1990. Why not invite back "overseas Japanese"—people of Japanese lineage who'd been born and raised elsewhere? They would be foreigners by passport, the planners assumed, but Japanese at the core. So programs and incentives were created for Japanese Brazilian workers to come be laborers in Japan.

The experiment had at best mixed results. It turns out those people with unbroken lines of Japanese descent had been changed by their families' many generations in Brazil. They had become, for lack of a better word, Latin. They stayed up late socializing, and they liked to samba. They barbecued meat in their cramped apartments, causing smoke damage. They didn't separate their garbage in the Japanese manner. They weren't particularly strict about rules, deadlines, timetables. The irony is that the Pakistani workers who'd been displaced by all this had, during their time as guest workers, been more Japanese than the Japanese Brazilians. The Pakistanis had been conscientious, diligent, respectful of communal norms.

A friend of mine named Leslie Helm told me this story. He's a former Tokyo correspondent for the *Los Angeles Times* and author of a book called *Yokohama Yankee*, about his own family's history in Japan. There are two ways to look at Leslie Helm: first, through the lens of his great-grandfather, Julius, a Prussian trader who opened up and built a commercial empire in the port of Yokohama; second, through the lens of his great-grandmother, a Japanese woman who was Julius Helm's mistress and, later, wife.

Most of the time most people see Leslie Helm as white. His face, his graying brown hair, his English first name and German last name all suggest some European blend. But look closely into his dark brown eyes, and you can glimpse a glimmer of Japaneseness in their shape. Talk to Leslie a bit, and he will admit that in subtle ways he is somewhat Japanese: in his deep knowledge of Japanese history and culture and perhaps in his own self-effacement, his quiet attention to the relational scheme of things. I half-jokingly declare that he is Overseas Japanese. But he looks away, his mouth turned in a sheepish, rueful half-grin. He is reluctant to admit his own sense of Japaneseness, not out of shame or self-hatred, but something quite different: unrequited affinity. The Japanese, he knows, would never count him as one of theirs.

There are today over three hundred thousand Japanese Brazilians who were brought to Japan as guest workers. But Japan's decade of recession has made the job market brutally tight, so after a generation living as guest workers in their ethnic homeland, raising families and creating a sense of place, they are now being "invited" to go "home." The Japanese government will pay them to be repatriated, covering air travel and offering a lump-sum bonus, on a single condition: that they never come back.

I am Han Chinese. That is pure Chinese stock. Blackest hair, fair-yellow skin, high cheekbones. The Han account for over 90 percent of China's population, making the other officially recognized ethnic minorities of that country, from the Hui to the Miao to the Zhuang and of course the Tibetans, something of an afterthought in the popular imagination. Beijing's method for subduing troublesome distant parts of the country in the

West, like Tibet and some of the Uighur and Mongol regions, is to export large numbers of Han people there. The indigenous population of these outer regions bitterly resent the arrival of the Han. The Han, not unlike the whites of the American West, come cocksure and ready to civilize the natives. The Han are good. The Han are bad. The Han are a tidal wave, washing away local diversity. The Han are progress incarnate. Like them or not, we all talk of "the Han" as a given.

The Han, however, are not a given. They are not some original clot of pure blood that existed before history and then diffused into circulation. They—we—were constructed, like any and every group that has ever thought of itself as a race. The idea of a proto-ethnic Han identity, separate from the civic identity of membership in the Chinese state, came to prominence during the late Qing Dynasty in the 1890s. Why? Because the Qing had been established by invading Manchus, and although these "barbarians" had been Sinicized after their arrival in 1644, the idea of the Han people—Hanzu—now became a way to split off the "foreign" minority ruling class from the mass of "authentic" Chinese.

In just the same way, "Overseas Chinese" is a fiction. As the cultural anthropologist Chris Vasantkumar has observed, many of the patriots who invented the Republic of China and who eventually toppled the Qing were living in exile, in Europe and the United States, where they developed an intellectual framework for Chineseness, a nationalism that could be said to have preceded the imperial dynasties. Sun Yat Sen, the father of the Republic, the one figure that Nationalists in Taipei and Communists in Beijing can agree to revere, was able to build support and funding for his revolutionary efforts by traveling a worldwide circuit of ethnic Chinese communities, from San Francisco and Honolulu to London and Tokyo. But Sun and reformers like him, notes Vasantkumar, "did not simply find 'Chinese' people abroad, draw on their natural patriotism, and yoke them effortlessly to the glorious cause of the Chinese nation-state." Instead, they had to sing and preach this spirit of commonality, this imagined homeland, into corporeal existence. These affinities "were thus the products of nationalist agitation and circulation, not their causes."

Thus was born the myth of Overseas Chinese. The Chinese term *Huaqiao* was a new national signifier that came into common usage at the turn of the last century. It was both a project of identity formation and the primary tool for executing that project. It gave the culturally and linguistically varied communities of Chinese ancestry around the planet something transcendent to belong to. It represented the step prior to "If you build it, they will come." It was "If you say it, they will build it." And they did. It was, in short, a Chinese Dream.

The opposite of prejudice is not tolerance, really; it is thoughtlessness. As in: "I never thought of you as Chinese." Or, "I never thought of you as Asian." Such words, typically said by white people, are typically said not in malice; indeed, they are meant to be affirming, inclusive, even comforting. They mean, "I never thought of you as not like me." But such words can represent a kind of empathy on the cheap. They can express a too-quick leap to the safety of colorblindness, skittering past zones of tension and potential conflict and the difficulty of reckoning with one's own position in the colored grid of advantage and disadvantage. It's whistling past the graveyard, a superstitious wish that if color is not acknowledged, then it will not haunt. What irritates me about being told, as I have been at intervals throughout my life, that someone never thought of me as Chinese is this: I am Chinese.

The empathy of the presumptuously colorblind, to be sure, is preferable to outright hostility. But better still, and more necessary, is the empathy of the color-conscious: the non-Chinese American saying to the Chinese American, "I always thought of you as Chinese, *and* I always thought of you as like me."

In the hierarchy of needs articulated by the psychologist Abraham Maslow, we humans begin with a basic set of physical needs (food, water, warmth), then move to security, from there to belonging (family, love, friends), self-esteem (recognition and respect), and finally self-actualization (creativity, pursuit of inner talent). As Americans we have our own set of identity needs; our own smaller hierarchies of how we are seen.

Here is mine:

I need to be seen not as an enemy.
I need to be seen not as an alien other.
I need to be seen not as white.
I need to be seen not as without identity or color.
I need to be seen as Chinese.
I need to be seen as American.
I need to be seen as Chinese American.
I need to be seen as myself.

To be seen truly is no common occurrence. In his 1960 essay "Princes and Powers," James Baldwin describes the scene at a conference in Paris where African and American Negro intellectuals have gathered to explore the cultural content of the pan-Africanism they wish to promote. One African, Leopold Senghor, earnestly cites Richard Wright's memoir *Black Boy* and describes the debt it owes to African symbols and forms of storytelling. Baldwin is not impressed. "In so handsomely presenting Wright with his African heritage," he writes, "Senghor rather seemed to be taking away his identity."

Heritage and identity. The two are often conflated, spoken of interchangeably, but in fact distinct. One is the chrysalis, the other the butterfly; one, seed, the other, fruit. The first is insurance against risk; the second is risk. Even if we provide for everyone a useable heritage, we have only barely begun to acknowledge the full flowering possibility of identity.

Listening to the preachers of an imagined continental identity, Baldwin grants that there probably is something African in *Black Boy.* And yet, he writes, "its form, psychology, moral attitude, preoccupations, in short, its cultural validity, were all due to forces that had nothing to do with Africa." I would more than grant—would claim—that there is something Chinese in me, in my own patterns of thought and expression. The question remains, though, what to make of it, how to fashion from it and many other sources an identity that works and that can evolve. I am called today to consider myself part of a great Chinese diaspora, to find my destiny in that heritage. I can answer the call only in part, and mainly in English.

In Chinese *tongbao* is a compound word that means "compatriot." *Tong* means *together* and *bao* means *uterus.* To be Chinese is, at the deepest level, a matter of blood relations, the coagulation of disparate histories into one. Now that those shared lines of descent seem globally ascendant, so many people of Chinese blood who live outside China feel at once far from the core and reanimated at the core. Distance (and power) makes the heart grow fonder. And perhaps purer.

And yet purity is a trick of the eye. To be American is, at the deepest level, a matter of mindset. Can we face that fact? Can we embrace it as our advantage?

When I was nearly thirty, I came down with a bout of appendicitis. I had never been so sick before, and my emergency surgery left me in a longer convalescence than I'd ever experienced. For the first time since I had learned to shave, I went weeks without shaving. This didn't mean much: it would probably take me a year to work up a respectable beard. Nonetheless, about ten days into my scruffiness, I took a peek in the mirror to see if my hollowed face was regaining its color. I was shocked to discover a different kind of color. Amid all my jet-black wiry whiskers now grew a few reddish ones. *What the hell?* I thought. I cannot overstate how disorienting this dis-Orienting was. Suddenly I remembered a bit of family lore. My mother's mother, my Po Po, had the maiden name Yu. The legend was that her ancestors—and mine—were direct descendants of the Mongol invader Genghis Khan, who conquered most of Eurasia and whose Chinese surname was Tie. After Genghis died, some of his descendants, fearing retribution from his enemies, erased half of the character for Tie and converted it—simplified it, in a sense—into a surname pronounced Yu. I had never taken that piece of lore seriously. After all, some 8 percent of Asian men apparently have Genghis Khan's genetic material. But now, as I looked at myself in the mirror, thinking I could no longer vouch for the pure Chineseness of this Chinese face staring back at me, I could only ask: Who is swimming, overseas, in my Chinese blood?

Lius in the News

John C. Liu: New York City comptroller, 2013 candidate for mayor

Liu Yu: author of *The Details of Democracy* and leading blogger on Weibo

Liu Hongsheng (1888–1956): industrialist and subject of the book *The Lius of Shanghai*

Liu Xiaobo: Chinese intellectual and dissident, Nobel laureate

Lucy Liu: actress

Liu Tong: pastor of Silicon Valley River of Life Church

Liu Zhijun: former Chinese rail minister charged with corruption

Goodwin Liu: associate justice, California Supreme Court

Liu Wen: supermodel

Liu Xiang: Chinese track star, Olympic gold medalist

Randall Liu: NFL spokesman

Joseph Michael Kai-Tsu Liu: runner who runs barefoot for charity

Liu Yifei: actress

Betty Liu: Bloomberg Radio host

Lily Liu: civic entrepreneur, founder of PublicStuff

LIU: Long Island University

Eric Liu: champion professional poker player

CHAPTER 4

Destiny of the Nation

I. Dream

1.

When I was a boy, I looked up to someone—literally. High on the shelves of our study, surrounded by heavy marble lion bookends, was a sober black-and-white portrait of an officer in the Nationalist Chinese air force. He was a general. He was my father's father. I never knew him except by his serious mien frozen in photographs. But I knew this: He was born in 1908 in Hunan Province. He was a farmer's son. He attended Whampoa Military Academy in Canton. He became a pilot. He fought the Japanese and then the Communist Chinese, through the 1930s and 1940s. He became the chief of staff of the first air force of the first Republic of China. He helped launch the Flying Tigers, the group of American fighter pilots who joined the Republic in the war against Japan. His name was Liu Kuo-yun: Liu, our family name; Kuo-yun, meaning "destiny of the nation."

No pressure.

He and my grandmother, Wan Fang Liu, had six sons. This was staggeringly auspicious. Their names were Chao-ning, Chao-hua, Chao-han, Chao-li, Chao-shiuan, and Chao-kai. The Chao in each name means "a portent" or, secondarily, "a million-fold." My father was the second son, Chao-hua. Hua is shorthand for the Chinese people. So my father was a "millionfold Chinese" or "portent of the Chinese."

My grandfather died several years before I was born. As a child I heard very few stories of him. We spoke of him so rarely that I didn't have a proper name for him. I came to call him Ye Ye only as I approached adulthood. Instead I referred to him only as "your dad" or "your Baba" in rare questions to my father: "Dad, did your dad like to play baseball?" I cannot recall a single telling anecdote about him at work or at home. All the photos of him are portraits, formal ones in uniform or semiformal ones with his family. As social convention dictated, he is unsmiling. I have never seen a candid shot of him.

I've been told that my grandfather was kind, even mellow, at least for a military man. It was his wife, my Nai Nai, who was especially gung ho and a relentless force. She raised six sons in wartime. She was born the year after the Republic was founded and is now over 102 years old and still fierce. My grandfather was more of a conciliator. He was fair. He was sincere and trustworthy. He had physical and moral courage. He was trusted by Chiang Kai-shek.

In one picture of him as a new cadet at Whampoa Academy all these traits are discernible. His eyes are not hard. He is not bloated with bravado. He is calm, earnest. His eyes are a little more heavy-lidded, his lips a little thicker, his skin a shade darker than that of the average Chinese. That facial phenotype is present, to varying degrees, in his sons. The brothers looked alike and generally like their father, especially uncles 1, 2, 3, and 5 (they addressed one another by birth order—Lao Er, second oldest, was my father). Uncle 4 had a flatter, more angular face, with jet-black hair swept across the forehead. As a *Star Trek* fan I came to think of him as "Scotty," because he looked to me exactly like a Chinese James Doohan, who played engineer Montgomery Scott. Uncle 6 was fairer and taller than the others, his face most like his mother's.

By examining this set of brothers I was able to piece together facets of their father, like a traveler across Europe divining from fraternal Romance languages the ancestral meter and grammar of Latin. Uncle 1—referred to by his brothers as Da Ge, or "big brother," and by us cousins as Da Bo, or "big uncle"—looked most like my grandfather and gave me a glimpse of my grandfather's own bearing and propriety. Da Ge truly was the big brother, the one who figured things out for the others and would clear the path in ways small and large. My father and Uncle 5 both had a mischievous streak, an impish glint in their eyes. But my father in particular could be harshly judgmental about what Lius did and didn't do, a trait I attributed also to his father. Uncle 3 was placid and reserved. Uncle 4 was earnest and more expressive. In Uncle 6 I could see the kind of ardor and intensity that must have propelled the son of a farmer to dream of taking flight.

In one sense, this attempt to imagine my grandfather—to deduce the theme by hearing only the variations—is foolhardy. My grandfather remains a mirage, a shimmering wave of guesses and reveries upon which I wish to impose a pattern. And yet. Whatever the genetic truth of the origins of this brother's solemnness or that brother's playfulness, however untraceable those biological claims may be, there is and always was a family truth, a truth of culture, of *nurture*, that made the inheritance of General Liu Kuo-yun something real and distinct. From these many brothers—and indeed, from the many more sons and daughters they bore—comes one imperative still: to fulfill the destiny of the nation.

2.

As early as I can remember I was fascinated by iconography. I loved fonts and symbols and became an obsessive student of insignia—of the armed services, of major league baseball teams, of the Cycle 1-2-3 dog food brand, of the World Wildlife Fund and its *Ranger Rick* magazine. I loved the shape of the words "STAR TREK" at the beginning of each episode. I loved the Starfleet badge and the lettering on the hull of the USS *Enterprise*. I sketched all those over and over again. I also loved the flag of the Republic of China, as Taiwan is called. I would draw and color it in constantly, trying to get the proportions exactly right. I got a shiny ROC flag sticker when I was in fifth grade, and I promptly affixed it to the black file cabinet that's been with me ever since.

Why did I love that flag so much? It was beautiful and simple, yes: red field, navy blue canton, white sun with twelve petal-like rays. But I loved it mainly because unlike, say, the flag of the People's Republic of China—the Communist mainland—it had the same colors and the same basic proportions as the flag of the United States. In point of historical fact that was mere coincidence. The founders of the Republic of China had very specific Chinese meanings for the colors and symbols: the blue is for Chinese nationalism; the white for democracy; the red, fraternity. But to my childhood imagination, the flag symbolized something deeply personal and fortunate: the integration and fusion of Chinese and American aspiration.

When I was a boy, I wondered what it would be like to deliver a nation. It never occurred to me to ask: Which nation? I understood that I was Chinese and that I was American. I did not yet understand that these were not the same thing.

With stories of my grandfather filling my boyhood daydreams, I imagined myself a Flying Tiger, and later a US Marine Corps fighter pilot, one of the Black Sheep squadron led by the roguish Colonel Pappy Boyington, himself a former Flying Tiger. I dreamed of getting into dogfights with Japanese Zeros. I dreamed of killing "Japs," and painting a little imperial Japanese "Rising Sun" flag by the cockpit of my blue Corsair every time I killed one. I dreamed that to be Chinese and to be American was to have the same enemy and therefore the same identity.

It wasn't until years later, when I learned about how Chinese Americans after Pearl Harbor took to wearing large buttons that proclaimed "Chinese, not Japanese," that I saw, as if out of body, the absurdity of my earlier self-concept: The Good Asian. The loyal one. But in my youth, it seemed not cringe-worthy but positively providential that I was Chinese rather than Japanese, and this state of being and not-being, this convergence of colors and overlapping of flags, shaped me and the self-story I made.

3.

In the months after Pearl Harbor, as the internment of Japanese Americans was under way, *Life* magazine printed a helpful visual guide for its readers. It was titled "How to Tell Japs from the Chinese." This full-page spread consisted of some prefatory text and two large photos, of a "Jap" face and of a Chinese face. With clinical detail, it diagrammed the differences: "earthy yellow" versus "parchment yellow" complexion; higher bridge versus flatter nose; never rosy-cheeked versus sometimes rosy; longer, narrower face versus broader, shorter.

You know which is which, right?

4.

When he was a boy, my father was frequently very sick. He read and read and read. He learned the Chinese classics. He missed a lot of school. While at home, he learned to drive a Jeep. This was in Taipei, where his family had fled in 1949, when the Communists took the mainland. He was thirteen.

The war had ended badly for Chiang Kai-shek and the Nationalists. But Taiwan became more than a last stand or temporary sanctuary after a frantic retreat. It became the ground on which the idea of a stable republican China would for the first time be proven. Over the course of the ensuing half century, even as Taipei lost diplomatic ground to Beijing, Taiwan became the seedbed for a new kind of China: prosperous, educated, and eventually free and self-governing. But at the time the Liu family landed there, it was a backwater still bearing the imprint of Japanese wartime colonization. The house my father grew up in had a dusty dirt courtyard with a few thin trees offering mere patches of shade. The house was built in the Japanese style, with tatami mats and sliding doors. It was spare and a little dilapidated. At the same time, in the pictures of those years and in the stories my father used to tell of his youth in Taipei, details emerge that reveal relative privilege. In one photograph, all six brothers are sitting, from shortest to tallest, on nice bicycles. The person who taught my father how to drive a Jeep was, it happens, the family driver.

This was the household of a general. And though my father's family, like other Nationalist Chinese families who had fled to Taiwan, endured austerity and hardships in those first years in their new land, my father and his brothers were of course among the lucky ones. They had an opportunity to dream of a new life, a new republic, and, ultimately, a new nation altogether.

II. Arrival

1.

Da Bo (Uncle 1) was the first to arrive in 1952. He enrolled at the South Dakota School of Mines and Technology. He was eighteen. Then came my father, in 1955. For the first few months he stayed with his big brother in Rapid City, working odd jobs to save money. One was painting the yellow line down a highway. Soon he set out to begin his own studies, ending up at the University of Illinois at Urbana-Champaign. Eventually, three other brothers would also earn degrees from Illinois.

They had immigrated to America upon coming of age because that was where anyone with talent and ambition was going in those years. Taiwan was laying the groundwork then for its postwar economic miracle, with careful planning and investment. But in the early and mid-1950s, only a few years after the exodus and at a time when it seemed war might break out anew across the Taiwan Strait, the infrastructure of opportunity was still underdeveloped. My grandfather made it clear that for college and beyond, his sons should study in America.

During those years, my father and his brothers, equipped with basic English, made their way to their North American campuses (Uncle 5 went to Canada). They wore slim suits and narrow ties and black horn-rimmed glasses. They made friends with other students from Taiwan, had picnics and weekend outings, the small community of them snapping black-and-white Kodak shots of each other. And as they worked hard and applied themselves, bachelor's degrees became doctorates and bachelors became husbands. Most of the brothers began, in ways not wholly intentional, to build an American life. They settled in Yorktown Heights and Wappingers Falls and Mattawan and Champaign. They had sons and daughters, the first coming in 1961. They took jobs at Bell Labs and IBM and the Illinois Geological Survey and the University of Illinois. They started in rented apartments, then moved into ranch and colonial houses in developments with names like Merrywood on streets called French Hill Road and Old English Way. They began to raise American families.

My father didn't seek US citizenship until 1978. I remember when he and my mother came home from their naturalization ceremony, bearing little American flags and booklets about the Constitution and about the meaning of citizenship. It wasn't until recently, when I came upon my father's certificate of naturalization among miscellaneous papers in a cardboard box, that I appreciated how prosaic the occasion must have been. By that time, the document merely confirmed what had gradually and imperceptibly become a truth: they had lived here too long not to call it home.

2.

When I was the age of my emigrating father and uncles, I had my own form of arrival. One humid mid-summer evening I stepped off a bus in rural Virginia with a sack of clothes, and into one of the most disorienting, frightening scenes I'd ever experienced. As soon as my feet hit the ground, large, burly men were screaming at me, shoving me, telling me to go this way and that. It was stressful. But I was arriving, quite voluntarily, into the US Marine Corps. For six weeks the summer after my sophomore year of college, and for another six weeks the next summer, I was at Marine Corps Officer Candidates School in Quantico, Virginia.

At OCS I became acculturated to an Anglo-American naval tradition and lexicon. They called arrival at the base "disembarkation." They called windows "portholes," the floor "the deck," doors "hatches," the right side "starboard," and the Marine Corps itself the Fleet Marine Force, or FMF. Those weeks marked a passage for me, a chance to connect my family history and military heritage to my claiming of *this* country. The echo of cadence calls, the roar of aircraft overhead, the clicking of boots, the mouthfuls of dust after fifteen-mile hikes, the bloat of hastily swallowed canteens of water, the chill of waking up in dark woods, the undulating contour maps: every aspect of my Quantico experience made me feel linked to what I imagined my grandfather experienced two generations earlier in the muggy, buggy marshes outside Canton. I also had something to prove at OCS. I was a little guy. A Chinese guy. An Ivy League guy. A guy with glasses. Indeed, that was the name the drill instructors gave me in the early weeks: Glasses. "*Glasses*! Get over here!!" "*Glasses*, are you *shittin'* me? What in *hell* do you think you are *doing*?!"

But as harrowing as OCS was at the start, I had been braced for worse. I was ready to hear "Chink" and "Gook" and "Ching-Chong" and other things I'd heard as a boy in upstate New York, only now with more malice and from the mouths of grown men against whom I could not possibly retaliate. I told myself to keep my cool when it came. It never came. The worst I got was when one day, while straining through interminable leg lifts, I saw a sergeant-instructor looming over me and sneering, "Look at you, little Liu. You're not a man. You're a *computer*. Aren't you good at computers? Isn't that what you do?" That was it. Tame. Lame, in fact.

I remember the moment later in that first summer when I knew I had made it. I was walking across the asphalt parade deck, on the way back to barracks. I was alone, not in formation, but I still strode purposefully, keeping my crisp Marine bearing. Suddenly a voice rang out from across the parade deck, startling me. "GENERAL LIU!" It was one of the drill sergeants, but not from my platoon. He and another sergeant, sitting on the steps of one of the classroom buildings, had been watching me march and were mightily amused. "Look at him go!" said one of them, imitating me with exaggerated strides and puffed-out chest. "He thinks he's a general already!" Instantly, I had to calculate. There was no hostility. This was friendly ribbing.

They knew my name. I smiled ever so slightly and kept walking, as purposefully as before. *General Liu*. I liked the sound of that.

3.

We spent many Christmases with Da Bo's family when I was in grade school. Usually my grandmother Nai Nai was there, the great matriarch with her commanding voice and her distinctive Hunan accent, which flattened vowels and gave words a sharper edge. Whenever she was there, all the brothers and their wives dropped their everyday Mandarin to match their mother's Hunan elongated enunciations and cadences. This must have been, for the brothers at least, the language of childhood and home. We would all crowd around a great circular dinner table, the lazy Susan filled with platters of spareribs and steamed fish and fried dumplings and Chinese greens. Cacophony followed.

After we'd slurped up the last grains of rice from our bowls, the kids would play Sorry! and Candyland while watching holiday specials in the basement playroom. We ate Wise potato chips and Chips Ahoy cookies. Upstairs, the adults ate orange slices and Chinese peanuts and date-nut candies and played mahjong and talked urgently about the state of things—their work, their families, the situation in Taiwan. When bedtime approached on Christmas Eve, we cousins would roll out sleeping bags by the large artificial Christmas tree, next to deep piles of gifts with little tags bearing our Chinese names. The curtains were drawn. The tangled tree lights cast faint, refracted primary colors across the living room. For a while longer the grown-ups moved about wordlessly, filling stockings and tidying up, their footfalls absorbed by the plush, tan, wall-to-wall carpeting. Soon enough their bedroom doors clicked shut, and all that could be heard in the house was the low soothing hum of the refrigerator in the kitchen.

It occurs to me only now that all the adult conversation during those holiday visits was conducted in Chinese, and all the cousin conversation in English. Nai Nai dominated the adult discussions. Though I couldn't follow all of it, I understood enough of the words and all of her tone. She was always pressing the brothers, pushing them to do more. To be more. She could be harsh and cutting. Her silences and sighs could be suspenseful. She had strong opinions about matters as large as the future of the Nationalists and as small as where to eat dinner.

My father, I now realize, didn't tell his mother or brothers very much about his end-stage kidney disease and his four-times-weekly home dialysis and his foreshortened life prospects. Even in the company of his birth family he did not roll up his shirtsleeves, lest they see the bulbous, scabbed fistula by his right wrist. As they strived to fashion a sensation of security for their children, my father and his brothers had little idea that in our second-generation hearts were being formed memories and associations, even if painful or distorting, that would bind us to this place and away from them, their ancestors and origins.

In the decades since, we the cousins have experienced accomplishment and recognition, things that could proudly be recounted at the big round table, but other things too, which Nai Nai would not so easily have found the words to discuss when we were young, or ever: things like divorce, estrangement, disease, simple disappointment. Things made in America.

III. Reckoning

1.

Most of the brothers earned PhDs, in chemistry and engineering and geology and mathematics. My father did not. He was impatient. He got his master's in math from Michigan, started working, thought about switching to law school, of all things, and then decided he would rather work. He got a job at IBM. In short order his managers realized he had unusual clarity of thought and expression, and was cool under pressure. He became a manager. He rose through the ranks. Every night he and my mother would spend hours during and after dinner deconstructing the corporate politics and maneuvering, their rapid-fire Chinese sprinkled with bureaucratese like "MVS/VM" and "line, not staff," and with names of coworkers like "Popovich" and "Ewing" and power centers like Raleigh and Somers and San Jose.

Uncle 5 had returned to Taiwan after getting his doctorate. All the others stayed, for decades. By any reasonable standard, they did well in America. They embarked on professional careers that rewarded their expertise. They became respected scientists and researchers in their disciplines. Three of them worked at universities. Two worked at IBM. Another worked at Bell Labs. But a question nagged: Was there more to this life than middle management or mere tenure? By the standards they held, and to quote a maxim from one of the management self-help books in my father's study, "good enough was not good enough." It seemed that too many of the men—the white men, the *yangren*—who were making decisions about the prospects and career paths of the Liu brothers did not appreciate their true talent and ability. What my father and uncles came to wonder, as their ambitions chafed against the grid of American institutional life, was whether their dreams might ever find full expression here in the United States.

Timing is everything. Just as several of the brothers began to feel this restlessness in the early and mid-1980s, Taiwan was coming into its own as an economic powerhouse. Taiwan was one of the Asian Tigers of that era that had recovered completely

from the devastation of war to challenge American in primacy. Taiwan had also finally ended martial law a plunging into the wild churn of democratic politics. Fre was in the air. A storyline of opportunity was unfurling wan was on the global competitive map, and its leaders looking to keep it there. So they began aggressively to rec Taiwan-raised talent—engineers and other experts—and lu them back from the United States. What they promised was n higher salaries, or higher salaries only. They promised a chanc to start or run great enterprises. They promised a chance to make history.

One after another, the Liu brothers heeded the call. Uncle 5, who'd been there for years already, ascended to the presidency of National Tsinghua University. Uncle 3 soon became president of National Central University. Uncle 1 took early retirement from IBM and became a consultant helping to create new high-tech industrial parks across Taiwan. Uncle 6, the youngest and perhaps most frustrated with corporate America, quit Bell Labs and started his own telecommunications equipment company in Taipei.

My father wanted to go too. But he was convinced he couldn't. To begin with, he didn't have a PhD. In the credential-obsessed culture of Taiwan, this felt to him like deep disadvantage. For another thing, there was the matter of his illness and home dialysis—all of which he had kept hidden from his colleagues, from our neighbors, from anyone not a blood relative. The complications of finding reliable care in Taipei, of being able to make arrangements that would preserve his desired secrecy, also seemed too great to overcome.

I remember a trip he and Mom took to Taiwan in 1990 to see Nai Nai. When they came back, I sensed an undercurrent of disappointment, regretful preoccupation. Then it passed,

or at least was submerged. And he resolved to go on climbing the IBM ladder. Every job there had a level number. As far as I knew, there wasn't another Chinese American during my childhood who attained his level number at IBM Poughkeepsie. But he never cracked the highest tiers. His last business card says "Project Executive." Not "Vice President." Not "Director."

In the years following the return of the other brothers, the Liu family became famous in Taiwan. Uncle 6's start-up company, Teco, grew into a conglomerate making everything from home appliances to wind turbines and operating retail phone stores and trendy fast-food chains. Uncle 3 led his university to prominence and was then tapped to lead Academia Sinica, the Taiwan equivalent of the American Academy of Arts and Sciences. Uncle 1 became a leading figure in Taiwan's economic and industrial development. And Uncle 5 alternated between university presidencies and leadership in government, serving as transportation and communications minister, then vice premier, and ultimately prime minister of the Republic of China.

All of them, through their work in business and culture and education and diplomacy, have become significant bridge-builders across the strait to China. And presiding over this spectacular array of achievement was their mother, my Nai Nai, Wan Fang Liu, proud and fierce widow of a great general, who had outlived almost all of the founding generation. Together they were celebrated as paragons of the revitalized republic. The sons, under the proud and watchful eye of the matriarch, had redeemed the promise of the patriarch's name.

But from an American perspective—from my perspective—this is equally a story of a nation's failure—*my* nation. The paths of the Liu brothers underscore three simultaneously true stories about many other Chinese Americans: first, they arrived

with more advantages of station and education than is typically acknowledged in model minority stereotypes; second, they worked and applied themselves relentlessly to earn their credentials; and third, they perceived glass ceilings that neutralized the first two factors. It used to be for Chinese Americans that wherever the ceiling here was set, it was still higher in absolute terms than what was possible in the ancestral homeland. It's not that way anymore. It hasn't been that way for going on a generation. The master narrative of American life holds that its magnetic pull, its promise and prosperity, is irresistible. That story, though, is disintegrating. America still mints immigrant PhDs, but these days it can't always keep them. A reverse brain drain is under way. The number of Chinese-born graduate students returning to China has increased 40 percent just since 2010.

You might think, hearing the tale of my uncles, that Taiwan was just a small pond where it was easier to be a big fish. But think of it this way: Taiwan has a population of twenty-three million, nearly twice that of Illinois, where so many of the brothers got their higher education, and a few million more than New York. Why, in the comparably small pond of New York State, or the even smaller pond of Illinois, couldn't Chao-han Liu (Uncle 3) see a clear path to leading a university? Why did Chao-kai Liu (Uncle 6) feel blocked from becoming a captain of industry? Granted, these are good problems to have. No one exactly felt sorry for my uncles for leaving secure careers in America in pursuit of still better ones. But the question that lingers is why America couldn't keep them.

2.

Life trajectories are hard to explain, still harder to anatomize. Chance plays a far greater role than any of us ever wishes to admit. Mere hard work, mere intelligence, sweat, and grit cannot always account for why some careers ascend, some descend, others never take flight.

My first boss, David Boren, then a US senator, once gave an unusual reading assignment to me and two other young staffers who, like Boren, had gone to Yale. It was a book called *Remembering Denny*, by Calvin Trillin. Denny Hansen was Trillin's Yale classmate, a handsome, genial godlike swimmer and Rhodes scholar, one of the biggest men on campus during the late 1950s. *Life* magazine covered his graduation. Hansen's years after Yale and Oxford, though, were a crushing accumulation of unmet expectations. He never figured it out. He could have done anything. He chose to be an academic, in a subfield that turned out to be "wrong." and out of favor. He grew irascible. He hid the fact that he was gay and never felt he could come out. He ended up committing suicide at fifty-five.

The message of the book, for us cocksure go-getters, was simply this: practice humility. The message of the *gift* of the book, from someone as distinguished as Senator Boren, was that no one is exempt from the forces of randomness that inevitably enforce humility. It was quite a gift.

Yet when I consider the various trajectories of the Liu brothers, who all had the same initial advantages and burdens of promise, and when I take into account the whims of fortune, bad and good, I do not in fact see mere randomness. I see a pattern in which correlation compellingly implies causation: those who left America did better once they left. It's a hard truth. There is a larger pattern at work today, for immigrants and the native-born alike. Social mobility in America has slowed. Put aside American Dream rhetoric. The strongest statistical predictor of whether you will be poor or rich in America is now this: whether your parents are poor or rich. Not education. Not character. Not even chance.

3.

My ardor for America is innate. More precisely, I am innately ardent about belonging to something greater than myself—namely, America. Had I been born and raised in Taipei or Beijing, though, I would likely be as proud a patriot of the Republic, or the People's Republic, of China. When I was nine, my Sunday Chinese school had a special movie screening. Folding chairs were set up in the elementary school gym the Mid-Hudson Chinese Association had rented. The place was packed. We kids sat on the floor in the front, craning our necks up at the screen. The film was called *Ba Bai Zhuang Shi—The Eight Hundred Heroes*. It was a war movie made in Taiwan, based on the true story of an overmatched battalion of Nationalist Chinese soldiers who held off a Japanese division at a famous 1937 battle in Shanghai. It was a thrilling, sentimental, action-packed movie. I cried at the end. If at that moment, my father had said we were moving to Taiwan so that our family could take its place in the line of heroes, I probably would have jumped up ready to go.

He didn't, of course. More than a decade would pass before he would consider it. By then, his children were Americans. Of course, that was technically true of all the cousins who'd grown up here. Uncle 4 had also stayed in America, working his entire career at the University of Illinois and becoming a beloved member of the community there. He was the only one of the brothers who gave himself a non-Chinese name: Jack. He raised daughters who would end up working for the Illinois State Police and Disney. *That's* American. But it's safe to say none of the cousins had become more ardently attached to this nation and its meaning. As I approached adulthood, I had zero interest in moving to Taiwan. If my father was torn about whether to stay or to make the leap, my self-centered preferences trumped his ambivalence; my certitude, his doubt. He stayed. And the current of life carried us all in the direction it had already been carrying us: deeper into America.

4.

When Uncles 4, 5, and 6 were teenagers, they became well known in Taiwan for writing a series of martial arts novels. Uncle 5, sixteen at the time, was the driving force behind them. He knew the conventions of such picaresque books, but he also knew his Chinese history, had been steeped in tales of bandits and heroes and warlords and emperors. The books tapped into all of that. They were best sellers, and the newspapers loved telling this story of three young sons of a leading family embarking on a creative adventure together. The books also made the brothers some money, enough for Uncle 5 to help pay for college.

Recently, after decades of service in politics and higher education in Taiwan, Uncle 5 returned to storytelling. He published a new series of martial arts novels set during a Ming Dynasty civil war. This series, too, got a lot of press coverage in Taiwan, but whereas the media narrative the first time was about precocious teenage authors writing under a pseudonym, the narrative this time was about an esteemed former prime minister returning, under his own well-known name, to his literary and civilizational roots. It is an arc as complete and fulfilling as can be imagined. It makes me imagine what my father's own arc could have been.

5.

I wonder sometimes why Dad was so captive to his preconceptions. Why did he convince himself that without a doctorate he could be nothing in Taiwan? That was a box he built. Why was he so intent on masking illness or weakness? This too was costly. Sometimes I think a real American would have said, "Who needs a PhD? I can make it anywhere!" A real American would have said, "Yeah, I'm sick. So what? I'll show everyone what I can do." But I know that's naïve. Americans are no less prone to keeping perceived weakness from public view (see: FDR and JFK). What, then, does it mean to be a real American? Is it a matter of simple longevity and familiarity and acceptance in this land? Or is it having the mindset of the perpetual immigrant, ever eager to start a second act, always willing to start over? In this latter sense, my father was perhaps never more American than when he first arrived, when he'd staked everything on an unseen promise and was ready to take on any risk. In the years that followed, life happened. His options narrowed, his attachments grew. It turned out he had not internalized the American spirit enough to leave America.

It has been twenty-two and a half years now since my father died. I was twenty-two and a half at the time. He is with me for fleeting moments every day, in how I laugh at an absurdity, or offer harsh judgments, or break down a problem, or sit in silence when I realize I've erred, or overplay corny jokes. But the older I grow, the thinner and more fragile the fibers of memory become, the more I must strain to imagine how he'd handle a situation. I offer my daughter a composite portrait of her Ye Ye that consists of my recollections. It's better than nothing, more textured than what I knew about my Ye Ye. But death deprives the living of the possibility of surprise. It precludes an unexpected departure from prior patterns. Might my father, one or five or ten years after his initial decision not to go back to Taiwan, have changed his mind? Might he at some point have deviated from his straight-line insistence on hiding his illness and his belief that illness would disadvantage him? We cannot know. Extrapolation fails. It is up to us to make our own jagged lines.

IV. Deliverance

1.

For years the Japanese house and dusty courtyard that the Lius moved into in 1949 remained the family home. With each passing decade, as Taipei boomed, the city crowded in around that house. The unpaved street in front became a four-lane boulevard. On all sides modern high-rise buildings sprouted. The old house, which the Nationalist government had provided to the widow of a national hero, remained stuck in time. Nai Nai ruled over it, and its constancy and her forcefulness had the effect of making my father and uncles, no matter how old or accomplished, always their mother's sons.

When Uncle 5 was a government minister in Taipei, he sometimes stayed in the old house, slept in the same room he'd slept in as a boy. The first time I visited Taipei, I stayed there too. It was 1992. I was part of a congressional staff delegation, representing Senator Boren. During that trip I and the other staffers were treated by the government like VIPs, feted at ten-course dinners and taken on tours. At the family home, my uncles, usually stoic, were unusually expressive in their love and support of me. My father had been gone only two years, and his brothers were filled with bittersweet pride to see me doing work of such seeming importance, pride amplified when, the following year, I began to work for an American president.

On my most recent visit, in 2011, much had changed. The old house had been torn down. In its place the government had erected a six-story apartment building, with one of the units reserved for Nai Nai. Her flat had modern amenities and a view of a twenty-first-century city, but the main thing was she was living on the same piece of land she'd lived on for over sixty years. She had just celebrated her 101st birthday. She was frail but still lucid and forceful in her speech. On this visit, I had no official business. I was a tourist, with my mother, my daughter, my partner Jená. One evening Uncles 5 and 6 took us out to dinner. In the nineteen years since my first visit, Taiwan had established itself. China was resurgent, and my uncles were confident contributors to this revival. What struck me most at dinner was how little interest they now took in America. The tone of their comments about American capitalism and politics was indifferent. America was not what mattered. The presidential campaign was not of great consequence.

The next afternoon, Uncle 6 took us to a cemetery on the outskirts of Taipei to visit the tomb of my grandfather. The stone tomb is substantial. It sits high on a hill, in the shade of well-manicured trees. It includes a carved inscription by Chiang Kai-shek in memory of Liu Kuo-yun. After my uncles had their successes in the 1990s and beyond, it became a well-known site. People came regularly from across Taiwan to see it and to pay respect to the father of this famous family. Other families built their own tombs in the same format, perhaps to absorb something auspicious by osmosis. On this day, though, it was just us: my mother, my uncle, my aunt, my daughter, my partner, me. I felt their eyes on me as I stood before the tomb and bowed deeply three times.

2.

In the years right after the Nationalist Chinese fled the mainland and retreated to Taiwan, the United States was their great defender. When the Communists in 1958 shelled the little islets of Quemoy and Matsu off the coast of Taiwan, forcing schoolchildren like my parents to do emergency drills to prepare for the expected invasion, President Eisenhower sent the US Navy into the Taiwan Strait. The shelling stopped. The invasion never came. Even after President Nixon normalized relations with Beijing and the People's Republic and de-recognized the Nationalist government in Taipei, the United States remained Taiwan's primary guardian and partner in education and investment. For decades, there was little to no interaction across the strait. To get from Taipei to Beijing, one had to fly through Hong Kong. But gradually, starting in the 1990s, cultural exchanges began; family reunifications proceeded; bans on direct investment and travel were eased.

Taiwan's position today in relation to China and America is not unlike that of Chinese Americans: in between, and pulled more strongly than ever by China. We—Taiwanese and Chinese Americans alike—embody the interdependence of the two civilization-states. We benefit from the inheritances and infrastructure of both. We broker exchanges between them, though increasingly on China's terms. The gravitational pull of China is especially palpable among my uncles, who in local parlance are "deep blue" (from the Nationalist Party or Kuomintang, against outright independence for Taiwan, for more bridge-building with the mainland).

So it is interesting, to say the least, for me to contemplate the idea of China as the enemy of my nation. No serious policymaker or commentator in the United States calls China an outright enemy. But nor does anyone call China an ally. Rivals, competitors, codependents: these two countries face each other warily and sometimes adversarially. From cybercrime to disputes over sea lanes and currency manipulation and human rights to accusations of military espionage, there is plenty in the US-China relationship that can lead to trouble—if not to hot war then to cold peace.

Does a Chinese American who calls for accommodation and cooperation with Beijing look to his or her compatriots like a stooge? Does a Chinese American who calls for bellicosity and containment of the Chinese threat seem to his or her compatriots like a self-hater? Does it matter how we *seem*? There were Japanese Americans after Pearl Harbor who were so-called no-no boys, protesting the policy of internment by declining both to pledge allegiance to the United States government and to serve in its military. There were also Japanese Americans who went straight to enlist, who served in the all-Nisei 442nd Regiment, one of the most decorated US Army units in World War II. They made different choices but honest ones, and both groups did indeed prove their loyalty to the *idea* of America.

After he stepped down as premier, Chao-shiuan Liu (Uncle 5) took on the job of running the General Association of Chinese Culture. In this role, he serves now as intellectual ambassador—keeper and explainer of a Chinese cultural inheritance. In a recent lecture he offered his thoughts on the choice China confronts as it grows mightier: whether to attain its goals by reason or by force. Reason, in his telling, means an appeal not only to abstract logic but also to the internal logic of Chinese civilization: the *li*, or rites; the texts and the unwritten norms that glue a culture together, that can transcend geography or geopolitics. Force means both arms and the throw-weight of money. Soft power or hard? How will China persuade? How will it win friends and influence nations? What will be the source of its appeal?

It's a good question for the United States as well. There have always been two entwined sources of our nation's appeal: the vision of America as a land of unbounded economic opportunity, and the promise of America as a land defined not by blood or ethnicity but by a race-blind creed of equality and liberty. We have often failed to live up to that vision and that promise. But what marks this country as exceptional is that we have always held it a betrayal of national purpose to fail, and have thus always strived to fail *less*. Now, however, as social mobility has slowed in America, the gap between our ideals and our actual conditions is growing perilously wide. It's an open question whether we can muster the will to close it.

This moment makes Chinese Americans a bellwether. Our prospects and our choices, here in America, will influence the balance of power, the polarity of appeal, between China and America. Chinese Americans today, whether of the first or second or fifth generation, are not all slotted into the pigeonholes that my uncles found so intolerable. There is the Chinese American fashion designer who makes the First Lady's dresses. The Chinese American novelist from Brooklyn who's written the next great Southern novel. The Chinese American avant-garde composer and performer who's upending electronic music. At the same time, apart from these headline-worthy outliers, in the classrooms where Chinese American students are still seen as mere grinds, in the boardrooms where Chinese American employees are still seen as followers rather than leaders, and in the backrooms where Chinese American workers are still seen as cheap obedient labor, stereotypes are not collapsing. They are still holding, holding us all back.

Who will protect us from *this* threat?

3.

Merit is the revered ideal of the American elite, and the motif of the morality tale of American success. But what if the morality tale is a myth?

Frank Samson, a sociology professor at the University of Miami, recently conducted a survey of white adults in California. He asked them their views on admissions to selective colleges and found strong support for the idea that admissions should be determined by "meritocratic" measures like test scores and GPA, regardless of race or ethnicity. This is consistent with the general view of most whites that affirmative action undermines the integrity of selective institutions. But when told prior to the survey that Asian Americans are proportionally twice as numerous in the selective University of California system as in the state population, the respondents changed their tune. Now they favored a reduced role for grades and scores and greater emphasis on "intangibles" like leadership and involvement.

"The results here suggest," Samson noted drily, "that the importance of meritocratic criteria for whites varies depending upon certain circumstances." Meritocracy, as long as it preserves my position. Meritocracy, unless it undermines my advantage. Talk about selective admissions. To the Chinese Americans who played by the rules of meritocracy in order to enter good colleges and professions, only to be passed over when the criteria for advancement became "leadership potential" and "people skills," this is not news. Merit serves at the pleasure of power.

4.

John Adams said, "I must study politics and war that my sons may have liberty to study mathematics and philosophy. My sons ought to study mathematics and philosophy, geography, natural history, naval architecture, navigation, commerce, and agriculture, in order to give their children a right to study painting, poetry, music, architecture, statuary, tapestry, and porcelain."

Think of Liu Kuo-yun as John Adams, studying war. Think of me, the grandson, doing the closest thing I can to architecture and poetry: writing books. It's a nice parallel, a cross-cultural statement of obligation, ever oriented toward making a better life for the sons. What Adams's little chronicle hides, however, is the fact that each successive generation's freedom to pursue a "higher" art or calling brings along with it a quantum of compounded, unearned advantage.

One way to interpret the story of my uncles and their migrations is to see it as a parable about meritocracy. They went where their talent was properly rewarded. But another is to see it as a parable about privilege. They went where their privilege could be leveraged. They were all immensely capable, even gifted. At the same time they grew up the sons of a general, members of the political-civic elite of their country. They started life with tremendous social and reputational capital, and with the networks and ability to tap networks, especially once they returned to Taiwan, that can be shorthanded as *guanxi*. It is true that none of them squandered his *guanxi* inheritance. But all of them did have one.

My own story is no different. I have worked hard all my life. I have achieved, and because of that I have been on occasion pointed to as a "model minority." But I was born with advantages. Though I didn't grow up wealthy, there was so much I could take for granted—starting with a family history of success and skill and even some glory. You can look at me and say I am proof of the ideal of equal opportunity and meritocracy in America: talent finding reward in the open market. But that's not quite right. What you can say also is that I—like many Chinese and Asian Americans who are cited as "overachievers" so that other minorities can implicitly be branded underachievers—began my American life with a nice allotment of opportunity. And I haven't blown it.

Amy Chua and Jed Rubenfeld, in their book, *The Triple Package*, say success is mainly a matter of culture. They'd argue that I, like other Chinese Americans, have a civilizational superiority complex, some status insecurity, and an ability to defer gratification—all because of my Chinese culture—and that this is why I've achieved. But culture is a coarse and deceptive filter. If it were true that Chineseness alone conferred this "triple package" advantage, then all Chinese Americans would be thriving. That's how it may seem in the popular imagination. But it's just not true. There are hundreds of thousands of Chinese Americans, and not just in urban Chinatowns, stuck in poverty or struggling to get a fair shot in life. The Chinese American poverty rate is higher than the average for Asian Americans—and higher than that of whites. Class matters. It matters profoundly. By ascribing primary importance to ethnic culture, one can easily—willfully—overlook the fact that the most powerful generator of poverty and disadvantage is poverty and disadvantage, and that wealth and advantage are similarly self-reinforcing.

The question for America is why more Americans, Chinese or otherwise, do not begin with an allotment such as I had—why access to opportunity is, indeed, narrowing. Deliverance of *this* nation in this century is not going to be measured by whether our GDP is greater than China's, or whether our blue-water navy is greater than theirs, but rather by the degree to which we manage to break up monopolies of opportunity in our own territory. This century's teenaged immigrants, landing on American soil, must not decide at midlife to go back from whence they came. This century's children of immigrants must not wonder at midlife whether their American Dream is a mirage. The mythology of meritocracy can make us think that our lots, good or bad, are simply what we've earned. But there is far more talent in America than is ever noticed or activated. Until that changes, none of us has truly earned a thing.

5.

Shortly after my daughter, Olivia, was born, Nai Nai came to Boston to see her. As Olivia napped, her little rose-petal mouth puckered into a shape I recognized: it was Nai Nai's mouth, exactly. In the years since, there have been many occasions when I've wondered how my small-framed daughter has such a big, forceful voice, with such a commanding, insistent tone. Then I remember: she is her great-grandmother's great-granddaughter.

It's difficult to imagine Olivia growing up in Taiwan or China. She's just such an American kid. But it's even more difficult to imagine what Nai Nai would have been like had she grown up in America. America in the early decades of the twentieth century did not reward vigorous, savvy, strong immigrant women of color. Even if that era's legal restrictions on Chinese immigration hadn't existed, even if she could plausibly have raised six sons in, say, the Chinatown of New York or San Francisco, what would Nai Nai and her husband have been? What kind of arc of opportunity could she have imagined for her family?

Then again, China in the early decades of the twentieth century wasn't generally great for a woman like Nai Nai either. Even in her station as the wife of a senior military officer, my grandmother's full range of ability and ambition never were fully expressed. And so I am led to imagine a country where it could have been. A place where she would have found glory not through the men in her family but wholly in her own right. A nation where her dreams could come to fruition not indirectly but directly. Can you imagine such a nation? I can. My daughter lives there now.

Counterfactual

I've always been drawn to counterfactual "what-if" history. I have two favorite works of such writing. The first is Philip Roth's novel *The Plot Against America*, in which Lindbergh beats FDR in 1932, accommodates Hitler, keeps America out of war, and ushers in a program of "friendly" forced assimilation and de-Judification of Jews in the United States. The other is Winston Churchill's little-remembered but ingenious 1930 essay, "If Lee Had Not Won the Battle of Gettysburg," in which he poses as a historian from an alternate time reflecting on the South's triumph in the Civil War.

These works prompt me to wonder: What if the Chinese Exclusion Act of 1882 had never been repealed? What if America had remained an essentially non-Chinese and non-Asian nation to this day? What if there were only a few hundred or thousand Chinese in America, instead of a few million? What would be the mindset of Americans now toward Chinese people?

Consider how Roth and Churchill each might have played with this question. Roth could expertly conjure up a fictional America sans Chinese people that in many respects would be similar to the one we know. That's what made *The Plot Against America* so chilling: how otherwise familiar and normal everyday life under a "softly" anti-Semitic Lindbergh administration seemed.

Churchill's approach, though, requires a double loop: we have to pretend to be someone (a historian from an America without Chinese people) who is trying to imagine an America *with* Chinese people. And this makes Churchill's method perhaps even more powerful than Roth's.

Try it. Get in the headspace of an American who has known only an America devoid of Chinese. Then, from that vantage, try to speculate about how Chinese people, had they had the chance to stay and get rooted here, might have influenced American cuisine, education, commerce, science, slang, culture. Try writing that essay as Churchill did, in the style of a detached scholar who now dares, as if it would be a radical act, to envision an America that wasn't so un-Sinicized. You could call the essay, "If Chinese Exclusion Had Ended."

Or, better yet, "If There Were Such a Thing as Chinese Americans."

CHAPTER 5

Letter and Spirit

All persons born or naturalized in the United States, and subject to the jurisdiction thereof, are citizens of the United States and of the state wherein they reside. No state shall make or enforce any law which shall abridge the privileges and immunities of citizens of the United States; nor shall any state deprive any person of life, liberty, or property, without due process of law; nor deny to any person within its jurisdiction the equal protection of the laws.

—Section 1, Fourteenth Amendment to the US Constitution, ratified July 9, 1868

1.

The Empire of China acts like a threatening cloud hanging over the virgin states of the Pacific. . . . Her people may swarm upon us like locusts. Their coming will unhinge labor, damage industry, demoralize the country, and by claiming and receiving the ballot may upturn our system of government altogether.

—Senator La Fayette Grover, Democrat of Oregon, March 2, 1882

How absurd would be the idea of undertaking to naturalize a Chinaman? When the question would be put to him, "are you attached to the laws and Constitution of the United States" what could be his answer? Why, sir, the whole proceeding would be a farce.

—Representative Horace Page, Republican of California, March 15, 1882

> *The Chinaman of twenty centuries ago is unquestionably the Chinaman of today. The operations of time, of climate, of foreign conquest, of emigration have made no visible impression upon his rooted national characteristics. He is original, immovable, and inveterate in the preservation of his race distinctions. He never amalgamates.*
>
> —Representative Addison McClure,
> Republican of Ohio, March 21, 1882

Perhaps the most striking thing about the 1882 debate in Congress over whether to ban Chinese from the United States is this: it is honest. The members of the House and Senate who harbored racial animus did not try to hide it. They candidly declared their disgust for the Chinese. They unabashedly, even eloquently asserted that whites were superior in every respect.

The debate proceeded in two stages over several months. First both chambers considered and passed legislation to ban the further entry of any Chinese for twenty years. President Chester Arthur vetoed the act, not because it was noxious race-based legislation but because the twenty-year term of exclusion went beyond the spirit of the treaty the United States had recently renegotiated with China, which had allowed for some constraints on the immigration of Chinese laborers but hadn't contemplated a generation-long ban. After a veto override failed, Congress went back to work for a second round, debating and approving a ten-year ban. This time the president signed the bill.

The Chinese Exclusion Act of 1882 was the culmination of decades of anti-Chinese violence, physical and legal: riots, racist ordinances, midnight roundups fueled by white resentment of the cheap Chinese labor brought in to mine our mountains and lay our railroad tracks. The Exclusion Act marked the first time in the history of the republic that we had banned a group by race from entering our territory, let alone from ever becoming citizens.

Note that I say, "*we* had banned." To which one might properly respond, "What do you mean, '*we*'?"

I often say it. We—America; Americans. We won the Second World War. We sent a man to the moon. We invented the mass middle class. But "we" cuts both ways, doesn't it? We enslaved Africans and barred them from citizenship. We betrayed, besieged, and beheaded tribe after tribe of Native Americans. We rounded up and interned Japanese neighbors. We excluded the Chinese. That is, *we* excluded *me*. We hated me. We blamed me for our troubles during the years of depression and labor unrest and social dislocation across this land.

There is so much packed into the casual "we." Of course, that's most obvious in the first three words of the Constitution. Just who are we, "the people"? Another notable aspect of the Congressional debate over exclusion, captured in Martin Gold's comprehensive history *Forbidden Citizens*, is that each side in the debate based its appeals on fidelity to the Constitution—and in particular, on the sanctity of American citizenship. Like the Lincoln-Douglas debates—which had taken place only twenty-four crowded years earlier—this was a contest over the founding principles of the republic and the basic question of who is "we."

Thus Senator Samuel Maxey of Texas: "The Constitution of the United States, in my judgment, never contemplated the bringing of people of all colors, climes, races, and conditions into the country and making them citizens. . . . The only people ever dreamed of to be naturalized citizens of the United States by the Framers of the Constitution or by the people of the states which ratified it were people of the Caucasian race." And to punctuate the point: "I trust that the refuse and dregs of the countless hordes of China will never find a welcome here."

Opponents of exclusion, like Senator George Hoar of Maine, responded that the bill at its very core was anti-American. The Constitution, he pointed out, contained provisions for uniform naturalization laws, not laws "which shall distinguish between races and between nationalities." The Fourteenth Amendment provided for birthright citizenship, and the Fifteenth protected against abridgments of the right to vote based on race or color. The essence of the American creed, the putative teaching of the Civil War, was that any contradiction or ambiguity in the founding documents should be resolved in favor of a race-neutral, universal freedom.

Other exclusion opponents, like Oliver Platt of Connecticut, pointed out that the anti-Chinese argument was a self-fulfilling prophecy: harassment and ostracization of the Chinese had prevented their assimilation; their nonassimilation then became the pretext for more harassment and ostracization. The exclusion bill was the natural culmination of such logic: unwelcome because excludable, excludable because unwelcome. And it played into the hands of the racists of the old Confederacy, who were happy to give the Western states latitude to mistreat and ban one kind of nonwhite so that they in the South might be more at liberty to oppress another.

In the end, voices like those of John Miller, Republican of California, prevailed. Miller had been a major general in the Union Army. He had fought at Shiloh, had chased rebels across Tennessee and Arkansas. He had bled for freedom. And after the war, when he became a California lawmaker, he had wielded the law in relentless persecution of the Chinese. To Miller, excluding Chinese was entirely consistent with fighting to end slavery. The Chinese had become virtual slaves in America, he reasoned. By disposition and physiology they worked like animals and were drawn into subhuman conditions of peonage. They were "unfit for the responsibilities, duties, and privileges of American citizenship. . . . If they should be admitted to citizenship, there would be a new element introduced into the governing power of this nation, which would be the most venal, irresponsible, ignorant, and vicious of all the bad elements which have been infused into the body politic, an element disloyal to American institutions, inimical to republican liberty, scornful of American civilization, and unfit to participate in the government of others."

That the support for exclusion was bipartisan—that men of the party of Lincoln should embrace race-hating laws so soon after the Civil War—was a measure of Reconstruction's failure. This was an era when white Northerners had tired of the cost of good intentions, had grown weary of the Freedmen's Bureau and of civil rights and the complexity of so much unfinished business; when white Southerners had sensed in this national fatigue an opportunity; when, as Du Bois put it, "Negro suffrage ended a civil war by beginning a race feud." White supremacy was to have a revival of legitimacy, by code and by custom, not only in the unreconstructed South but on the virgin Pacific Coast as well and in the grimy cities of the North.

The Chinese Exclusion Act was signed into law by President Arthur on May 6, 1882. It was made more stringent in 1884 and again in 1888. It was renewed for ten more years in 1892. It was renewed again in 1902, indefinitely.

A year after exclusion first was enacted, Denis Kearney was in New York City to generate support for his cause. His cause was race hate. An immigrant from Ireland and a rough-hewn sailor who'd settled in San Francisco, Kearney was the voice and face of the anti-Chinese movement. He'd begun his American career as hired muscle to help put down striking workers and their sympathizers, but he soon realized there was more fame to be won agitating against capitalists and the Chinese "coolie labor" they'd imported to drive down wages. An incendiary speech-maker with a rolling brogue, he held forth in an empty lot by City Hall and came to fame as "the sandlot orator." His orations often ended in a refrain heard in riots across the West: "The Chinese Must Go!" Kearney helped found the Workingmen's Party of California in 1877 and hijacked the state's constitutional convention in 1878, filling the charter with provisions to bar Chinese from voting and from being hired by California corporations.

In his classic study *How the Irish Became White*, Noel Ignatiev described the way Irish immigrants in the nineteenth century, who began at the bottom of the East Coast urban hierarchy alongside blacks, managed to climb their way up and claim their Americanness: by showing the WASP power structure in word and deed that they, too, were willing to trample blacks. The same story, substituting yellow for black, obtained in California. The Irish made themselves insiders by leading the stigmatization of the most marginal of the outsiders. Among the beleaguered scattered settlements of Chinese in the United States, Denis Kearney was feared and reviled.

But by 1883, Kearney was already in decline as a political force. His party didn't have money or infrastructure. With exclusion already achieved, he no longer commanded attention as a demagogue. He'd traveled to New York hoping to find patrons and political allies but found few. Instead, on July 18, a hand-delivered letter arrived at his hotel from one Wong Chin

Foo, publisher of a newly created newspaper called the *Chinese American*. In the letter Wong invited Kearney to engage in a public debate of "the Chinese question." The letter pulled no punches:

> I belong to the most ancient empire on this globe. You, by your own statements, belong to the most dependent and ill-treated nation of serfs ever deprived of its liberties. The flag of my country floats over the third greatest navy in the world. Yours is to be seen derisively displayed on the 17th of March in the public streets and triumphantly hoisted on an occasional gin-mill. The ambassadors and consuls of my nation rank at every court in Europe with those of Russia, Germany, England and France. Those of your race may be found cooling their heels in the lobbies of any common council in which the rum-selling interest in politics predominates. The race which I represent is centuries old in every art and science. That of which you are the spokesman apologizes for its present ignorance and mental obscurity with the plea that your learning and literature are lost in the mythical past.

Kearney, notes historian Scott Seligman, "could see no percentage in a face-off." He dismissed the challenge. But Wong had already let the papers know about it. He soon wrote, and shared with the press, another even more provocative letter challenging Kearney to a duel, adding, with a wink, "I would give him his choice of chopsticks, Irish potatoes or Krupp guns." Kearney again tried to swat away the irritant, telling a reporter, "The Chinese question is a dead issue, and I don't propose to spend time in discussing it now. . . . I'm not to be deterred from this work by the low blackguard vaporings of Chin Foo, Ah

Coon, Kee-Yah, Hung Fat, Fi Feng or any other representative of Asia's almond-eyed lepers."

Wong had referred to China in his first letter as "my country." But his actions, his status, and the name of his own newspaper belied him: he was American, a Chinese American original—and, in a sense, the original Chinese American. The excellent Seligman biography of Wong, *The First Chinese American*, indicates that he was the first to use that label in print, and had used it quite intentionally, even reversing the order of the characters in the Chinese name of the paper so that it would read *Chinese American* and not *American Chinese.* He possessed, in his feisty letters and his penchant for what today would be called "sound bites," full command of the English language. He had a thoroughly American instinct for public controversy and publicity stunts. He had deep knowledge of the government, laws, and politics of New York, California, and the United States.

And he had American citizenship. He had been brought to the United States at fourteen by a missionary family in 1861. In 1874, he hustled his way into a court in Grand Rapids, lied about his age, bypassed a two-step paperwork process, and on that very day became one of the first Chinese immigrants to be naturalized as a US citizen. Throughout his life as a citizen, he looked his country in the eye and told it what he saw. As a polemicist and itinerant public speaker, he became renowned, initially purely as a curiosity—this Celestial who could speak and argue in American English—and then, perhaps, as some kind of harbinger, of a future few could imagine. He cut off his queue and adopted Western dress, but he published controversial broadsides against the missionaries, who, in his view, were enablers of imperialism in his native land. "Why Am I a Heathen?" he asked, in his most famous essay, denouncing Christians for all the sin and exploitation they had visited upon

China in the name of the Lord. He started the Chinese Equal Rights League to seek to overturn Chinese exclusion. He wrote for *Harper's* and other national periodicals. He got involved in local party politics.

In 1887, four years after his first attempt to engage Kearney, he finally got his man. Kearney, by now a confirmed has-been and desperate for publicity, agreed to a public debate sponsored by the *New York World*. Papers from across the country sent reporters to cover the contest. What a Chinese American today notes about all the coverage is how favorable it was toward the nonwhite combatant—not just uncondescending but admiring. At one point, Kearney averred that he had nothing against the Chinese as a race; he simply opposed Chinese immigration because all Chinese had been brought "under the slavery contract system." The *Fitchburg Sentinel* noted archly that "anyone who has read Mr. Kearney's speeches will at once see what a new and pacific departure this was from his usual line of talk" and continued the blow-by-blow dispatch:

> "That is not true," said Wong, briskly. "You cannot prove that. Can you show me one Chinaman that was brought to America on contract?"
>
> "They all are," said Dennis [*sic*].
>
> "I wasn't brought here on contract," said Wong, warming up to his work. "I'm an American citizen."
>
> "The federal decisions are against that," put in Dennis.
>
> "I beg your pardon, they are not," was Wong's calm reply. "I'm an American citizen, and I've voted for the good old Democratic ticket and sometimes for a good Republican. The Federal decisions you speak of are wrong and unconstitutional if they forbid the naturalization of Chinamen. They must be admitted to citizenship, as I was fifteen years ago,

> by the provisions of the constitutions made by our forefathers, and—"
>
> "Your forefathers," exclaimed Dennis, wrathfully, "sure, what had your forefathers to do with it? Nothing at all. You can't call the framers of the constitution your forefathers. Hah!"
>
> Wong smiled wrathfully, but coolly, and said, "I call them my forefathers because politically they were."

What makes Wong Chin Foo so remarkable is his fearlessness. Whereas other Chinese in America then were voiceless, he was a loudmouth; whereas other Chinese in America had learned from both the old country and the new to keep their heads down, he picked fights at every turn, gleefully. Some immigrants were Chinese in America; he was Chinese American. Wong propelled himself through the otherwise impermeable membrane that in his day had kept all but a few people of Chinese descent entirely out of the arena of public life. Wong Chin Foo was a late nineteenth-century character Mark Twain could have built a picaresque novel around: restless, democratic, ever shedding layers, always with a showman's knowing look. He was a crusader, in some ways a loner, but he broke through. He lived like a citizen.

2.

It's the late 1990s, nearly forty years after my mother's arrival in America. She has been a widow for a few years. She has painstakingly rebuilt her life. She has managed to convert a mid-level job at IBM into a more significant one at the giant defense contractor that acquired her division of IBM. She needs security clearances in order to do this new job. She has to take a lie detector test.

My mother is earnest, without guile or pretense. Somehow she fails the lie detector. She fails it again. She gets nervous, can't sleep. Her blood pressure goes up. It has never come down. That was fifteen years ago. Eventually she passed, and she was cleared to do the work. But I for one never forgot the anxiety of that period.

Maybe that's because around that time, another Chinese American of her generation also failed a polygraph. He too had come to the United States via Taiwan to get educated and became a scientist. His name was Wen Ho Lee. He worked at Los Alamos National Laboratory, a government nuclear research center in New Mexico. He was quirky. He was quiet. He didn't talk much. Someone got it in their head that he was passing secrets to the Chinese, who had made sudden and surprising weapons advances. He stood accused by his peers and by fellow citizens. He was detained for nearly a year in solitary confinement.

I remember once being told by Norm Mineta, the former commerce secretary under both President Clinton and President George W. Bush, about the way the government had categorized him after Pearl Harbor and just before he was herded to an internment camp. On the forms he was made to fill out were two categories: "Alien" and "Non-Alien." He asked, "What's a Non-Alien? Isn't that supposed to say 'Citizen'?" No one answered.

In times of doubt and anxiety, some citizens can slip into an ambiguous status called "Non-Alien," a holding pen of sorts. Just ask Wen Ho Lee, who, yes, had been sloppy about taking home some documents he shouldn't have but who fundamentally was not a spy. His life and name and career were all destroyed by a two-year witch hunt that played out in the media.

What my mother experienced, when she failed her polygraph, had nothing to do with suspicion of espionage. But her experience made me realize that with her face and accent and history, she might always be presumed foreign until proven otherwise. Not so Chinese but not quite American. In between, perpetually.

Excerpts from the interrogation of Wen Ho Lee by FBI agents in Santa Fe, March 7, 1999, as reported in *My Country Versus Me*, Lee's memoir, authored with Helen Zia:

AGENT: Look at it from our standpoint, Wen Ho. Look at it from Washington's standpoint. . . . You have an individual that's involved in the Chinese nuclear weapons program. And they come to your hotel room, and they feel free and comfortable enough to ask you a major question. . . .

LEE: Uh, mmm.

AGENT: And then in 1994, they come to the laboratory and they embrace you like an old friend. And people witness that, and things are, are observed, and you're telling us that you didn't say anything, you didn't talk to them, and everything points to different than that.

LEE: Well . . . (sighs).

AGENT: So, you know, I mean, it's, it's, it's an awkward situation that I, I can understand, you know, where, where these things could happen. I mean, you were treated very nicely in 1986 when you went to China.

LEE: Uh, hum.

AGENT: I mean, they were good to you. They took care of your family. They took you to the Great Wall. They had dinners for you. Then in 1988 you go back and they do the same thing and, you know, you feel some sort of obligation to people, to talk to them and answer their questions. . . .

LEE: No, no, no.

AGENT: You gotta understand this is the way it is. . . . You're being looked at as a spy!

LEE: Yes, I know. I know what you think, but all I'm saying is, uh, I have never say anything classified. I have never say anything.

AGENT: It might not be that, Wen Ho. It might not even be a classified issue. It might just be something that was said, but Washington is under the impression that you're a spy. And this newspaper article is doing everything but coming out with your name. I mean, it doesn't say anything in there that, that it's Wen Ho Lee, but everything points to you. People in the community and people at the laboratory tomorrow are going to know. That this article is referring to you. . . .

LEE: Let me ask you this. OK? If you want me to swear with the God or whatever, OK? I can swear if that's what you believe. I never tell them anything classified. I never told them anything about nuclear weapons. . . .

AGENT: You are a scientist, a nuclear scientist. You are going to be an unemployed nuclear scientist. You are going to be a nuclear scientist without a clearance. Where is a nuclear scientist without a clearance going to get a job?

LEE: I cannot get any job.

AGENT: You can't! Wen Ho, you gotta tell us what went on in that room. You gotta tell us why you're failing these polygraphs! Washington is not going to let you work in a laboratory or have a clearance!

LEE: I can retire, to tell the truth, I'm fifty-nine and something . . .

AGENT: You know what, Wen Ho? If you retire and the FBI comes in later on down the road. A day, an hour, a week, and we come knocking on your door, we have to arrest you for espionage! Do you really think you're going to be able to collect anything?

LEE: No, no, but look, look, look. . . .

AGENT: They're going to garnish your wages. . . . They're not going to give you anything other than your advice of rights and a pair of handcuffs!

LEE: But, but . . .

AGENT: And now, what are you going to tell your friends? What are you going to tell your family? What are you going to tell your wife and son? What's going to happen to your son in college? When he hears the news . . . "Wen Ho Lee arrested for espionage." What's that going to do?

LEE: But I'm telling you, I didn't do anything like that. I never give any classified information to Chinese people. I never tell them anything relating to nuclear weapons, uh, data or design or whatever. I have never done anything like that.

AGENT: Pretty soon you're going to have reporters knocking on your door. They're going to be knocking on the door of your friends. They're going to find your son and they are going to say, you know, your father is a spy?

LEE: But I, I'm not a spy. . . .

AGENT: Do you want to go down in history? Whether you're professing your innocence like the Rosenbergs to the day that they take you to the electric chair? . . . Do you want to go down in history? With your kids knowing that you got arrested for espionage?

LEE: I don't . . .

AGENT: The Rosenbergs professed their innocence. The Rosenbergs weren't concerned either. The Rosenbergs are dead.

LEE: I'm just telling you. I believe truth and I believe honest, and I know, I know myself, I did not tell anything . . . OK? I told you more than ten times . . . eventually something will be clear-cut, OK?

The space between can be killing. In the cold waters of San Francisco Bay, not far from Alcatraz, is a smaller outcropping of rock called Angel Island. It is the little-known negative of Ellis Island. On Angel Island was a clapboard prison, created in 1910 to execute the policy of Chinese exclusion. Four years earlier the great fire in San Francisco had destroyed all immigration records, enabling Chinese immigrants to evade the Exclusion Act by claiming to be the "paper sons" of Chinese men already lawfully in the United States but whose records had been lost in the fire. Immigration officers were thus suspicious of every entrant. Until 1940, Chinese newcomers trying to disembark in San Francisco were detained at Angel Island, given often humiliating physical examinations, and then subjected to lengthy, detailed, even surreal interrogations.

Q: Did you ever see your father?

A: I saw him when I was a little boy and we have a big picture of him at the home.

Q: Did you ever see your paternal grandfathers?

A: No, neither of them. They died a long time ago.

Q: Did your father have any brothers or sisters?

A: Yes, four brothers including my father and one sister.

Q: How many of those are living?
A: Two living and two dead.
Q: In what house?
A: The same house with us.
Q: What is the location of your house?
A: 4th row 4th house.
Q: Where does Jew Mun Jew live?
A: Not far from our house.
Q: Same row with your house.
A: No, not on the same row.
Q: Toward the tail of the village?
A: Near the tail of the village.
Q: Did Jew Fook ever sleep in a house near you?
A: Yes, a long time ago.
Q: Where was that house located?
A: The 4th house on the 4th row.
Q: That is the same location given for your house, isn't it?

These were a few of the questions posed in 1918 to a thirteen-year-old boy named Jue San Tong. The policy of the immigration service was that all Chinese should be "presumed excludable until proven otherwise." That presumption became, in practice, a presumption of mendacity. The goal was to force the detainees to betray themselves and their "alleged" family members, to expose their fabrications. Each detainee was forced into a dizzying maze of memory.

Q: How many steps exactly from one bedroom to another?
Q: Was the clock metal and hung on the wall or wooden and set on the mantel?
Q: Did the second uncle live in the fourth house or in the fifth?

Q: Had the marriage of an aunt been conducted in the traditional way or not?
Q: How many times did your father write to you last year?
Q: Does your village face north or west?
Q: What is your name?
Q: What are your other names?

Whether their answers were real or fabricated, whether the anchors of their entry were phantom or quite corporeal, the detainees were equally poorly treated. They languished for weeks and months, sometimes even years, on Angel Island. Some committed suicide by hanging themselves in their cells or, in one notable case, ramming a chopstick into an ear. Others simply waited. They had no papers, or even paper. So into the wooden and cement walls of the compound, those earnest emigrants carved Chinese characters, stroke by clear stroke, Chinese poetry composed in rough classical form, lamenting their limbo as they stared out helplessly across the water at America.

今日為冬末，
明朝是春分。
交替兩年景，
愁煞木樓人。

Jin ri wei dong mo,
ming zao shi chun fen.
Jiao ti liang nian jing,
tou sha mu lou ren.

Today is the last day of winter,
Tomorrow morning is the vernal equinox.
One year's prospects have changed to another,
Sadness kills the person in the wooden building.

Today busloads of students every week take the ferry across the foggy bay and disembark at Angel Island. They walk the compound, run their fingers through the etched characters in the walls. Students are given assignments to reflect on the poems, to imagine being coached for an interrogation, to search out their own families' records of arrival and processing. Some will reflect later on the lesson. Some might even tell their parents about the experience. Most will not. Most will step back on the ferry and return through the mists and live out the deep irony of our liberty: that in America we are free to forget, that only in America does the phrase "That's history" mean that something need no longer be remembered.

3.

It's the start of Constitution Week in mid-September. I'm in Philadelphia, in a vaulting glass and steel building called the National Constitution Center. Sitting next to me is Benjamin Franklin, getting ready for his speech. Jefferson is somewhere nearby; I just saw him. I look out the window and see a parade of Americans in Revolutionary Era garb with militia colors flying. They are marching across the mall from Independence Hall. They are the Sons of the American Revolution, each man a lineal descendant of our founding generation. They are here to celebrate the 225th birthday of the Constitution.

As the Sons stream in with their spouses, many of them Daughters of the American Revolution, they look like a group that has a routine for events like this. What they don't realize is that in a few minutes, some Chinese guy is going to be leading them in a ceremony they didn't sign up for and aren't sure at first whether to like. To the Sons and Daughters of the Revolution, American citizenship is like a birthright.

But what few people know is that it took a Chinaman to make American citizenship an *actual* birthright. His surname was Wong, although he was American-born—and that would prove to be crucial. In 1890, eight years after Chinese exclusion was enacted, a cook named Wong Kim Ark left San Francisco, the place of his birth, to visit relatives in China. When he returned, he was denied entry, on the idea that he was a Chinese subject to exclusion. He argued—or, rather, his white lawyers argued—that the language of the Fourteenth Amendment's citizenship clause was plain: all persons born or naturalized in the United States are citizens of the United States. Though his parents were Chinese nationals and though the law barred any more Chinese from entering the country, Wong Kim Ark had been born in the United States. His case made its way up the federal courts, and eight years later, thirty years after the ratification of the Fourteenth Amendment, the Supreme Court ruled in his favor.

The Court didn't do so out of a love of the Chinese. There was much antiquarian futzing about in the majority opinion, unearthing ancient precedents from the Saxon tribes of middle Europe and parsing the etymology of the word "jurisdiction." But in the end the text of the amendment was immovable, and to read it against the Chinese would be, in the words of Justice Horace Gray, "to deny citizenship to thousands of persons of English, Scotch, Irish, German, or other European parentage who have always been considered and treated as citizens of the United States." *That* wouldn't do. And so, in *United States v. Wong Kim Ark*, a race-blind principle of birthright citizenship became the law of the land—and it happened because a Chinese American had exercised his right to seek remedy in a court of law. To test whether America was a nation of its word.

Joseph and Mary Tape were a remarkable American couple. They were pioneers—he an immigrant from China (born Jeu Dip) who started as a milk deliverer and hustled his way into building a thriving business helping other Chinese immigrants navigate American bureaucracy; she a Chinese girl from darkest Shanghai sent to America on a contract of indentured servitude who had run away from her procurers, had ended up in a home for orphans and former prostitutes, had taken the surname of the matron of the home (Mrs. McGladery), had made herself a respectable wife, and now kept an upright Victorian household. They raised their children in a middle-class San Francisco neighborhood, away from Chinatown, counting as friends many prominent whites. At the same time, they were involved in Chinese community associations and spoke out against the very discrimination that made brokers like Joseph necessary (and prosperous). They were among the first Chinese American couples in America to live life as a Chinese American couple, integrated yet not wholly isolated from their roots. But when it came time for their seven-year-old daughter Mamie to begin school, they were utterly shocked when she was barred at the schoolroom door.

The year was 1884. Congress was further tightening the ban on Chinese; Wong Chin Foo was tangling with Denis Kearney. Wong Kim Ark was working in a restaurant in Chinatown. In her subtle biography of the Tapes, *The Lucky Ones*, Columbia University historian Mae Ngai describes how in this period norms and expectations about the visibility and voice of Chinese people were in flux. It was possible for Chinese Americans to live in the very epicenter of the anti-Chinese movement and to use the law, the sword being wielded against them, also as a shield to protect them. Mamie Tape—"That Chinese Girl," as one headline put it—had been turned away from a school where white girls and boys were being educated. Her parents protested to the school board, but that body and the state's superintendent of public education had firmly upheld the customary and statutory ban on any "Mongolian" child in the San Francisco public schools. The Tapes hired a lawyer, who called Mamie's exclusion a blatant violation of the Fourteenth Amendment's guarantees of equal protection and due process. The Superior Court agreed, and the California Supreme Court affirmed in March 1885.

Hurley v. Tape today stands as a historical highlight of anti-anti-Chinese litigation, part of a vast tapestry of such cases woven throughout the mid- and late-nineteenth century by many more litigants and advocates than contemporary Americans realize. Chinatown mutual aid associations typically funded the litigation, sometimes with support from Chinese consulates in cities like San Francisco, and enlightened white members of the bar typically represented the plaintiffs. Some cases, like *Yick Wo v. Hopkins* (ordinances designed to put Chinese laundries out of business, even if race-neutral on their face, are invalid if discriminatory *as applied*), are cornerstones of modern constitutional law. Many others are unknown except to legal historians. The index of *In Search of Equality,* Charles McClain's classic study of anti-Chinese law in California, lists dozens of such cases from this period:

Ah Chong, In re
Ah Din, People v.
Ah Fong, In re
Ah Hee v. Crippen
Ah Hund, Welch v.

Ah Ping, In re
Ah Pong, Ex parte
Ah Quan, In re
Ah Sing (Case of the Chinese Waiter)
Ah Wing, In re
Ah Yup, In re
Awa, People v.
Baldwin v. Franks
Case of the Twenty-Two Women
Chae Chan Ping v. United States
Chew Heong, In re
Chin Ah On, In re
Chin Ah Win
Chin Yen, People v.
Chin Tow v. United States . . .

And yet the Tapes' victory was in two senses ambiguous. First, the school board had anticipated an unfavorable ruling and as a practical matter bypassed it by creating within the public school system a separate school for "Chinese and Mongolian" children. So although white taxpayers would now have to fund Mamie's education, at least their children wouldn't have to partake of it. This stratagem would later be enshrined by the 1896 *Plessy v. Ferguson* ruling, in which the Supreme Court held Jim Crow's "separate but equal" scheme to be a valid form of equal protection.

But the bigger reason why the Tapes' victory was ambiguous is that, as Ngai astutely observes, their argument had rested in part on the claim that they and their children were not actually very Chinese. They had claimed in their depositions that their daughter had had only white playmates since she was a toddler, didn't dress like other Chinese, would "look just as phunny amongst them as the Chinese dress in Chinese look amongst you Caucasians." Joseph was a Christian and had cut off his queue fifteen years earlier, and they took formal family portraits together "in the American costume." They were, in sum, the very model of a would-be white family.

This, of course, was a devil's bargain—a claim that their assimilation should trump their ancestry, that their choice of white cultural norms should outweigh their unchosen genotype. It was a gambit not uncommon in their times, this declaration, in Ngai's apt phrase, "of mistaken identity." Homer Plessy, the African American passenger barred from a white train car in Louisiana, had himself made the double argument that a whites-only segregation policy violated his equal protection rights as a black man and that, moreover, he didn't look black.

Sometimes courts were silent on the question of just how colored a plaintiff was perceived to be. Other times, they weighed in with great certainty about the demarcation of race and caste, opining that a South Asian, though Caucasian, could not possibly be white, or that someone a quarter black was irredeemably black. In Mamie's case, the court was silent on the Tapes' not-really-Chinese claim, basing its ruling entirely on equal protection grounds and state law. But in the Tapes' earnest brief were all the tensions of being the most liked of the despised: an unstable oscillation between claiming to be, on the one hand, Americans who happened to be Chinese and, on the other, Americans in spite of being Chinese. This was an age when thesis and antithesis sat side by side without any imminent prospect of synthesis. It was an age when "equal protection of the laws" could be at once sanctified and defiled. Mr. and Mrs. Tape, in reaching to transcend their Chineseness, underscored it; in asserting their Americanness, redefined it. Securely insecure, they are every Chinese American's progenitors.

4.

A sampling of the headlines in the *New York Times* about Wen Ho Lee, from March 6, 1999, through October 4, 2000:

BREACH AT LOS ALAMOS: A SPECIAL REPORT; CHINA STOLE NUCLEAR SECRETS FOR BOMBS, U.S. AIDES SAY

U.S. FIRES SCIENTIST SUSPECTED OF GIVING CHINA BOMB DATA

AN EARLIER CHINA SPY CASE POINTS UP POST–COLD WAR AMBIGUITIES

THOUGH SUSPECTED AS CHINA SPY, SCIENTIST GOT SENSITIVE JOB AT LAB

CHINA SPY SUSPECT REPORTEDLY TRIED TO HIDE EVIDENCE

SUSPECT IN ATOM SECRETS CASE PUBLICLY DENIES AIDING CHINA

LEE'S DEFENDERS SAY THE SCIENTIST IS A VICTIM OF A WITCH HUNT ABOUT CHINA

SCIENTIFIC GROUPS COMPLAIN TO THE ATTORNEY GENERAL ABOUT TREATMENT OF WEAPONS SCIENTIST

FILES IN QUESTION IN LOS ALAMOS CASE WERE RECLASSIFIED

JUSTICE DEPT. REPLACES TOP PROSECUTOR IN NUCLEAR SECRETS CASE

DISCRIMINATION INQUIRY BEGUN AT WEAPONS LAB

FBI AGENT GAVE FAULTY TESTIMONY IN WEAPONS CASE

ACCUSED SCIENTIST TO GO FREE ON BAIL IN LOS ALAMOS CASE

JUDGE DOUBTS U.S. CLAIMS AGAINST SCIENTIST

A VANISHING SECURITY CASE

JUDGE ATTACKS U.S. CONDUCT

CLINTON CRITICIZES OFFICIALS' ACTIONS AGAINST SCIENTIST

RENO ORDERS INTERNAL INQUIRY INTO HANDLING OF SECRETS CASE

OFFICIALS DISAGREE ON HOW LAB SCIENTIST BECAME SPY SUSPECT

At a glance, this list of headlines suggests an arc—of betrayal, then of redemption; from accusation to exoneration. What a list like this does not capture, though, is the relative size, space, and placement—on the page and in the civic psyche—these various headlines occupied at various times. There was a straightforward progression: as time went on and the explosiveness of the initial headlines proved illusory, as the administration began to backtrack, the headlines shrank, and the stories fell off the front page.

Wen Ho Lee spent nine months in pretrial solitary confinement. He was nearly sixty when his detention began. He had been a naturalized citizen of the United States for twenty-five years. He was kept in shackles for all but one hour every day. Still, he fought the system. He had lawyers and advocates combating the media-political shadow conspiracy to smear him. He sued the federal government. He sued the newspapers.

In the end, every charge but one was dropped. He accepted a plea agreement in which he admitted to mishandling of sensitive documents and was sentenced to time served. The newspapers paid him a settlement to end his litigation against them. But that news was a whisper compared to the screams of disloyalty that had introduced him to his compatriots. And the only apology at the end of his case came not from his persecutors in the justice system or at the *New York Times* but from the federal judge in the final ruling on his case—Judge James A. Parker, appointed to the US District Court for the District of New Mexico by President Ronald Reagan in 1987. Judge Parker said:

> Dr. Lee, you're a citizen of the United States and so am I, but there is a difference between us. You had to study the Constitution of the United States to become a citizen. Most of us are citizens by reason of the simple serendipitous fact

> of our birth here. So what I am now about to explain to you, you probably already know from having studied it, but I will explain it anyway.

The Judge went on to explain why the unjust detention and harassment by the administration was unlawful, unjust, and, in his words, saddening.

> I am truly sorry that I was led by our Executive Branch of government to order your detention last December. Dr. Lee, I tell you with great sadness that I feel I was led astray last December by the Executive Branch of our government through its Department of Justice, by its Federal Bureau of Investigation and by its United States Attorney for the District of New Mexico, who held the office at that time.
>
> I am sad for you and your family because of the way in which you were kept in custody while you were presumed under the law to be innocent of the charges the Executive Branch brought against you.
>
> I am sad that I was induced in December to order your detention, since by the terms of the plea agreement that frees you today without conditions, it becomes clear that the Executive Branch now concedes, or should concede, that it was not necessary to confine you last December or at any time before your trial.

And then, noting that he had "no authority to speak on behalf of the Executive Branch, the President, the Vice President, the Attorney General, or the Secretary of the Department of Energy," Judge Parker apologized on behalf of the US judiciary system. In his book, Lee recounts turning to his lawyer at that moment and asking in a whisper whether this was what a judge typically did. "No, Wen Ho," came the reply. "This is very, very rare."

WHEREAS in the opinion of the Government of the United States the coming of Chinese laborers to this country endangers the good order of certain localities within the territory thereof:

Therefore, Be it enacted by the Senate and House of Representatives of the United States of America in Congress assembled, That from and after the expiration of ninety days next after the passage of this act, and until the expiration of ten years next after the passage of this act, the coming of Chinese laborers to the United States be, and the same is hereby, suspended; and during such suspension it shall not be lawful for any Chinese laborer to come, or having so come after the expiration of said ninety days to remain within the United States.

—From H.R. 5804 (1882), prime sponsor: Rep. Horace Page (R-California)

WHEREAS these Federal statutes enshrined in law the exclusion of the Chinese from the democratic process and the promise of American freedom;

WHEREAS in an attempt to undermine the American-Chinese alliance during World War II, enemy forces used the Chinese exclusion legislation passed in Congress as evidence of anti-Chinese attitudes in the United States;

WHEREAS in 1943, in furtherance of American war objectives, at the urging of President Franklin D. Roosevelt, Congress repealed previously enacted legislation and permitted Chinese persons to become United States citizens;

> *WHEREAS Chinese-Americans continue to play a significant role in the success of the United States; and*
>
> *WHEREAS the United States was founded on the principle that all persons are created equal:*
>
> *Now, therefore, be it Resolved,*
>
> *SECTION 1. ACKNOWLEDGEMENT.*
>
> *That the House of Representatives regrets the passage of legislation that adversely affected people of Chinese origin in the United States because of their ethnicity.*
>
> *SEC. 2. DISCLAIMER.*
>
> *Nothing in this resolution may be construed or relied on to authorize or support any claim, including but not limited to constitutionally based claims, claims for monetary compensation or claims for equitable relief against the United States or any other party, or serve as a settlement of any claim against the United States.*
>
> —From H.Res. 683 (2012), prime sponsor: Rep. Judy Chu (D-California)

5.

Sometimes progress can be measured by the kind of caricature a subject earns. A hundred and fifty years ago, newspapers commonly carried sketches of Chinese-as-vermin: pigtailed rats packed into filthy conditions and spreading vice. Sixty years ago, as the yellow hordes of Red China poured across the Yalu River into Korea, pop cultural images of the Chinese as menacing enemy proliferated. Fifteen years ago, in the midst of hysteria about "Asian money scandals" and secret Chinese donors infiltrating the presidential campaign-finance system, new-fashioned cartoon images of sinister, bucktoothed coolies appeared on national magazine covers.

So when in 2011 Goodwin Liu was painted in the press merely as a careerist, left-wing radical, temperamentally unfit to serve on the federal bench—without any additional insinuation that his Chineseness made him a danger to our republic—one could think, perversely, *Look how far we've come! In America today a Chinese American, as readily as anyone of any race or background, can now be demonized and taken down in national public life simply for narrow partisan reasons!*

I am not related to Goodwin Liu, though I do consider him a friend. I also consider him the embodiment of the meritocratic version of the American Dream. His parents were immigrants from Taiwan, physicians recruited here to work in underserved areas during the Vietnam era. Born in Augusta, Georgia, Goodwin grew up in Sacramento. He didn't learn English until kindergarten because his parents hadn't wanted him to adopt their accent. He became high school valedictorian, went to Stanford to study biology and follow his parents into medicine, won a Rhodes scholarship, and at Oxford decided instead to study philosophy and to pursue the law.

From there, his listless slacker ways came to an end: Yale Law School; a US Supreme Court clerkship with Justice Ruth Bader Ginsburg; a stint in the Clinton Education Department; a professorship and then associate deanship at Boalt Hall, the law school at the University of California, Berkeley; an active role in the Obama campaign and transition; and then a 2010 nomination to become a judge on the US Circuit Court for the Ninth Circuit. A buzz of expectation emerged—not at all generated by the unassuming, introspective nominee himself—that he would soon be in position to make history and become the nation's first Chinese American justice of the Supreme Court.

Then politics intervened. Republicans had also picked up on the buzz, and they found this picture-perfect Chinese American utterly threatening—to their generation-long efforts to keep the high court tilted rightward. They also sought retribution for Democratic filibusters of several of President Bush's judicial nominees. And they wanted a way to bruise the new president by proxy. So began an excruciating process of inquisition and obfuscation in which everything Goodwin Liu had ever said or written was used against him in a court of public opinion.

Conservative senators, abetted by relentless bloggers, searched out academic articles that Goodwin had authored. One was titled "Rethinking Constitutional Welfare Rights." That, literally, was all many on the right needed to read. They depicted Goodwin as a radical socialist whose views were out of step with the mainstream. They took his comments from a panel discussion about reparations to imply that he would force all nonblacks in perpetuity to pay compensation for slavery. They trumpeted testimony Goodwin had offered in 2006 against the nomination of Samuel Alito to the Supreme Court, in which some of his language was admittedly more heated than judicious, and made him out to be a slashing party apparatchik. Then they took the fact that Goodwin initially submitted an incomplete list of his many speeches and writings as proof that he had something to hide. The indignation of his opponents was breathless and theatrical, the kind of baroque affectation by which Washington makes small things big and big things small. Goodwin had many allies on the outside pressing his case (I was one). But the traditions of judicial nomination meant that he had to be exceedingly mild in his own defense. The Republicans filibustered his nomination to death in 2010. President Obama resubmitted it in 2011. The Republicans again filibustered, until the nomination was at last withdrawn later that year.

Goodwin Liu is American enough to be used and spiked as a political football. *Nothing personal*, you can imagine some of the

GOP senators thinking as they performed. But here is another way that Goodwin is all-American: he got a second act. On the afternoon his nomination died in the Senate, California governor Jerry Brown called him with an idea. Today Goodwin Liu is an associate justice of the California Supreme Court, the very body that in the 1854 case of *People v. Hall* had barred Chinese from testifying against whites on the grounds that if these backward inveterate liars were admitted to the witness stand, they would soon be "at the polls, in the jury box, upon the bench, and in our legislative halls." Indeed.

You might not guess it by her manner, but Ai-jen Poo has a tiger tattoo high on her right arm. You might not guess it because her manner is soft and kindhearted, her voice and lilting cadence as pacifying as a meditation tape. And if you judged her by her manner, you would not be the first to learn later just how much you had misjudged her.

Ai-jen Poo is the daughter of immigrants from Taiwan. Her father, a scientist, was active in the push for more democracy in Taiwan. Her mother and grandmother have been models for her of moral courage and strength of will. But Ai-jen had not been particularly groomed in her youth to exercise voice and power. She simply had an awakening. When she was a college student, she got involved in protests and sit-ins that resulted in the creation of an ethnic studies center on campus. From then on, she has been an organizer and national activist without peer. Her work has focused on organizing women in the low-wage economy, particularly domestic workers: nannies, maids, servants, caregivers. She created the National Domestic Workers Alliance, a network of dozens of local affiliates, and her innovative approach to collective action is at the vanguard of a nascent reinvention of organized labor beyond the format of traditional unions.

The women she organizes are most often immigrants, people of color, and desperately poor. They work and struggle in a shadowy quarter of economic and civic life that she likens to the Wild West: unregulated, exploitative, obscured. The historian Jean Pfaelzer, in her fine book *Driven Out: The Forgotten War Against Chinese Americans*, tells of a Chinese woman named Yoke Leen who marched into the Sonora, California, courthouse in 1910 to file an affidavit including her name, physical description, photograph, and declared status as a free native-born Californian—in the event she should someday be abducted or pressed into indentured servitude. It may shock some Americans to know that the same underground system that Yoke Leen was insuring herself against, or that brought young Mary Tape to America in the mid-nineteenth century, still exists in the early twenty-first. That's especially true for undocumented immigrants, who are especially vulnerable to wage theft, abusive working conditions, sexual advances, and worse. The Domestic Workers Alliance tells harrowing stories of such women to lawmakers around the country. Ai-jen has become savvy at deploying the media to generate pressure and at lobbying behind closed doors to direct it. As a result, multiple states have now passed a Domestic Workers Bill of Rights.

Ai-jen's method, though, is not about shock or shame or shrillness. It is about love. There is an audacity of love that Ai-jen Poo embodies and makes contagious, an audacity that makes cynicism turn in on itself and unfold as belief. She led one campaign in which families that hire domestic workers went hand in hand with their help to lobby for more legal protections for domestics. Her latest civic venture, one that in a sense subsumes all her other activism, is called Caring Across Generations. Its aim is to encourage the "gray tsunami" of aging Americans, who are disproportionately white, to find common cause with their caregivers, who are disproportionately not white. Its aim is to tell a new story in which self-interest is mutual interest, in which the content of our caring is more significant than the color of our skin, in which America learns to revere elders and therefore to revere the people who look after the elders. It is, though Ai-jen Poo might not say it this way, a more than passingly Chinese undertaking. It is also an enterprise as utopian and fantastical as America itself.

6.

Today there are some extreme right-wingers who would throw Wong Kim Ark and his legacy overboard. They live in fear that undocumented immigrants are crossing our border from China and Mexico to have so-called anchor babies on American soil, babies who presumably would then allow untold streams of blood relatives to join them here. They would repeal the Fourteenth Amendment's guarantee of birthright citizenship. Their motives are despicable. But the would-be repealers do prompt a thought experiment. What if being born here *weren't* enough to guarantee citizenship? What if we *all* had to earn it?

So there I was in Philadelphia, two days before the 225th anniversary of the Constitution, standing before two hundred Sons of the American Revolution. To be a Son or Daughter of the American Revolution requires some serious genealogy. It requires a serious revolutionary-era wardrobe. And most of all, it requires a serious commitment to extending the line, nurturing history, embodying it, reenacting it.

This is conservatism in the most literal sense: conserving the mark and meter of the original. There is something to be admired about people who are willing, in this country of transience and impermanence, to dedicate themselves to preserving the memory and identity of the founding. But citizenship is not a museum piece nor an object to revere. It is lived and revivified by the new as well as the old. New voices speaking the old scripture. New blood coursing through the old vessels.

I had come to Philadelphia to conduct something called a Sworn-Again America ceremony. When naturalizing immigrants become citizens, they go through an elaborate process. They take a test. They hear words from the American creed. They swear an oath to this country. So my collaborators and I thought, *Why not create something comparable for* everyone, *whether citizens of long-standing or new Americans, whether here with the proper documents or not, to recommit?* To renew our vows to America and become *sworn-again*. So we created a simple ceremony that concludes with an oath:

I pledge to be an active American
To show up for others
To govern my self, to help govern my community
I recommit myself to my country's creed
To cherish liberty as a responsibility
I pledge to serve and to push my country:
When right, to be kept right; when wrong, to be set right.
Wherever my ancestors and I were born,
I claim America
And I pledge to live like a citizen

I asked the Sons and Daughters to stand and repeat each line after me. They did, tentatively at first. Not all of them would look me in the eye as we stood there facing each other. I kept a brave face and spoke loud and clear with a smile. By the end, as they realized there was nothing untoward or subversive about this ritual, their voices carried more conviction. Afterward, two of the Sons approached me, their faces serious. I was braced to justify myself or at least to humor these men in tricorn hats as they explained their discomfort with my contrived new tradition. Instead one of them took my hand and thanked me. "You've got to keep doing this," he said in earnest. "All around the country." The other, teary-eyed, simply nodded in assent, repeatedly, as if not to me but to a voice within.

As manners make laws, so manners likewise repeal them.
—Samuel Johnson

Writing about "The New German Question" in the *New York Review of Books* and whether that nation will be able or willing to be a true magnet for global talent, the historian Timothy Garton Ash once observed, "Germany lags behind France and Britain, let alone Canada and the United States, in emitting those vital, elusive social and cultural signals that enable people of migrant origins to identify with their new homeland." Which raises the question: Just what are those vital, elusive signals?

They are social norms. They are found in the subtle way people look at each other. They are measured in the response that is evoked when people of migrant origins speak or stand in public view. They can be divined in what everyday conversation in small groups reveals to be acceptable or normal or at least tolerable. They are the little contagions of courtesy or discourtesy, regard or disregard, civility or incivility that bloom constantly across the contours of any community. Laws are in many ways merely the institutional deposit of the ebbing and flowing tide of such oft-unspoken attitudes. Yet if the current were to flow in only one direction, from custom to legislation, then racial segregation and the criminalization of homosexuality and Chinese exclusion might still stand. Laws decidedly change norms. Laws can and do emit vital signals.

The apology that Congresswoman Judy Chu drafted and championed is an exhibit of the interplay of law and norms. It is, in essence, a moral document. It names wrongdoing and apologizes for it. At the same time, the document has special force because it takes the form of law. It is not a press release. It is not a Facebook post. It is not a letter from members of Congress signed on gold-seal letterhead. Nor is it the Magnuson Act of 1943, the wartime exigent by which exclusion was summarily repealed. The whereases and thereforebeitresolveds of House Resolution 683 give it the shape of an official act of government—by our representatives, gathered in Congress—when it is in fact and effect ultimately a symbol. But symbols matter, powerfully. The House apology is designed to evoke the awe that law uniquely can evoke but not to be taken functionally as law. We are reminded of that by its Section 2, the incongruous disclaimer tacked on because some readers of the resolution who are not attuned to the history and the moral import of the symbolic act might otherwise take it as a basis for legal action. The disclaimer is the fine print appended to a contract of recognition and regret.

What the exclusion apology also highlights is the fluctuating distance between first- and second-class citizenship. Just as light is both particle and wave, citizenship is both law and norm. Chinese Americans throughout the history of the nation have—contrary to stereotypes of passive, stoic, silent victims—been active, assertive, and litigious in claiming and securing equality under law. And yet so many still feel the shadow of subordination and second-class treatment and the chill that the shadow casts. This is why, three decades on, the case of Vincent Chin retains such a hold on the imaginations of so many Chinese Americans. Chin was the Michigan man beaten to death with a baseball bat by a white autoworker and his son in 1982 who, blaming the travails of the auto industry on Japan, assumed Chin was Japanese. His killers, after a plea bargain and lenient sentencing, spent not one day in jail. This was a hate crime. But in 1982 there was no such category under law as a hate crime. There was only something timeless: injustice. Though killings like Chin's never became epidemic, his death was and remains totemic. It warned all Chinese Americans that they were still susceptible to fully lawful injustice.

What separates, then, the letter and the spirit of the law? Only convention. What is the difference between first class and second class? Only the difference we think of as normal. Only what we think of as *us*: who speaks for us, who advocates for us, who embodies us. Judy Chu is the first Chinese American woman to serve in Congress. She represents a district near Los Angeles that is roughly equal parts Asian, Hispanic, and white. She sits on the House Judiciary Committee and the House Small Business Committee. She spends most of her days helping constituents navigate federal bureaucracies, meeting with interest groups, showing up at town meetings, sitting in committee hearings on intellectual property or home foreclosures, proposing and sponsoring bills. Her nephew, Harry Lew, was a Marine in Afghanistan who fell asleep at his post, was hazed and punished relentlessly for three hours, and killed himself minutes later. Now she is fighting to curb the culture of military hazing, an endeavor she knows will depend as much on changing the norms of the armed services as much as the regulations.

Whereas: This is America.

Therefore, be it resolved.

The Iron Chink

One of these is true:

a. Bao-Li "Bobby" Chang was one of the first Chinese Americans to play professional baseball in America (and still one of the few ever to play). Though he never made it to the major leagues, the diminutive infielder established a record for durability, appearing in 983 consecutive games between 1922 and 1930. His achievement was overshadowed, of course, by the Yankee Lou Gehrig, the so-called Iron Horse. But Chang, among his farm club peers on the Peoria (Illinois) Chiefs, was affectionately called "The Iron Chink."

b. Chinese immigrant fish-butchers worked the canneries of Alaska and the West Coast starting in the late nineteenth century. When a fish-butchering machine was created in 1905 to simulate the effectiveness of Chinese laborers and replace them, it was dubbed "The Iron Chink."

c. In Locke, California, one of the last surviving towns established by turn-of-the-century Chinese immigrants, a thirty-two-year-old resident named Jen Cheong came up with an idea in 2010 to boost tourism. She started a triathlon to be run in the environs of Locke, along the Sacramento River. In a nod to the Ironman races, she gave it the name "The Iron Chink Triathlon."

CHAPTER 6

Performance

1. Roles

A note to Chinese American actors. Available parts today include:

Sage
Crone
Cook
Detective
Sidekick
Assistant
Spy
Doctor
Nerd
Intoxicated nerd
Scientist
Wife
Mother (Tiger)
Vixen
Mogul (foreign)
Gangster (foreign or domestic)
Martial artist
Warrior (enemy, if contemporary)
Villain
Peddler

Parts not available at this time (please check back next week/month/generation):

Romantic lead
Scamp
Action hero
Wiseass
Loveable loser
Detestable loser
Addict
Sitcom dad
Team captain
Ship's captain
Talk radio shock jock
Cop
Plumber
President

Is Charlie Chan really still the most well-known Chinese in America?

In the 1990s, activist Jessica Hagedorn published an anthology titled *Charlie Chan Is Dead*. This yellowface, pidgin-speaking Hollywood character embodied every kind of condescension, exoticization, and ventriloquism that self-determining Asian Americans were by then determined to throw off. But by 2010, author Yunte Huang, an immigrant from China and an English professor at UC Santa Barbara, had revived the icon in a best-selling history, *Charlie Chan*. In Huang's new take, the aphorism-spouting detective—based on a true-life, bullwhip-cracking Chinese American detective from Honolulu—was actually an admirable model of wisdom, tenacity, integrity, and effectiveness at a time when popular culture had either nothing or nothing nice to say about Chinese Americans. The "anti-Chan clan," as he put it, hated the stereotype they thought Charlie represented but had not looked closely enough at the books and films to see that he was in fact much more complex.

I admit I enjoyed some of the "Charlie Chanisms" Huang collected in an appendix: "Action speak louder than French." "Caution very good life insurance." Or, "Mind, like parachute, only function when open." But as the traditionalists, revisionists, and antirevisionists debated Huang's book and Charlie Chan's legacy, all I could really think was: *Who cares?* Charlie Chan, honorable or detestable, belongs to another century. I never read a Charlie Chan book, never watched a Charlie Chan movie, never was pricked by a malicious Charlie Chan reference. That his significance is now contested is perhaps a sign of enlightenment, but the contest itself is backward-facing. Who is the *new* icon? What is the new Chinese American character everyone in America will know, will imitate, admiringly or mockingly, about whom we can all have new arguments? Dead or alive, Charlie Chan is still too much with us.

We Americans absorb, half-consciously, an endless tide of image and narrative. Clips, sound bites, trailers, ads, hashtags, slogans, icons, poses—millions of microperformances, the raw material of myth and imagination. Sometimes stories come to us fully formed. Sometimes they are mere fragments, bits of narrative DNA floating through the primordial soup until by chance they bond with other fragments into lengths of code. These stories are all around us, the air we breathe and the water we drink, seeping into our psyches, telling us, reminding us, *making* us who we are. A conjured community. A nation.

One afternoon at the Missouri State Fair a rodeo clown can put on a rubber Barack Obama mask, and the rodeo announcer can bait the crowd into a frenzied call for the bull to gore the clown, for the thick rubbery lips of the clown's Barack Obama mask to get trampled. What scenes do the algorithms of our collective cultural memory call up? Klan rallies in midsummer. Billie Holliday singing "Strange Fruit." But also: Borat, the reckless fool from Kazakhstan (played by Sacha Baron Cohen) in the eponymous mockumentary. Here is Borat, a special guest at an actual Virginia rodeo, improvising a version of the Kazakh national anthem to the tune of "The Star-Spangled Banner" that ridicules America as a country of "little girls." The fearless Cohen never breaks character, not even when the crowd, unaware of the hoax, grows surly and starts raining boos down on him.

Now envision a different afternoon, just a few weeks after the Missouri State Fair, when the actual Barack Obama, wearing a somber mien, stands before the Lincoln Memorial facing a throng on the Mall for the fiftieth anniversary of Dr. Martin Luther King's speech at the March on Washington. Multitudes contain multitudes. The scenes from our memories and the scene before us merge; one tableau black-and-white, another, in living color: it's mythic, epic.

It's like a really good commercial.

And what is my place in such tableaux? Every time I see an Asian face on TV, I make a note of it. I enter it into a mental ledger, silently entering each new instance in the credit or debit column. My daughter pokes fun of me for this unremitting tally. A scarcity mentality, I suppose, is always a little funny, a touch foreign, to those who've grown up in relative plenty. There are certainly many more Asian faces on TV now than there were when I was her age: a Best Buy sales associate helping Amy Poehler buy gadgets, a couple test-driving a Honda, a young woman daydreaming about an LG phone. My daughter sees people like herself when she watches television—certainly more than I did when I was growing up. She sees other images that amuse and distract her—a smooth-talking African American centaur selling deodorant or proliferating clones of a nondescript white guy selling Dairy Queen ice cream or Buzz Lightyear whirling around in Spanish mode. She is imagining a community, a country, where someone Asian is simply part of the polychromatic mix.

That's the thing, though: *someone Asian*. It is a persistent social fact that to the average nondiscerning non-Asian, most East Asian nationalities, looking roughly alike, are interchangeable. A performer of Chinese or Japanese or Korean or Vietnamese descent can be asked to stand in for someone of any or all of those ethnicities. Or someone of a genericized pan-ethnic *yellow* category. Add that, then, to the list of allowable roles for Chinese Americans: Someone Asian.

Whiteness is the unspoken, invisible default setting of American life. We frame our conversations about race in terms of how white people see and what they think they see. We imagine that nonwhite Americans want to be more like white Americans. We imagine that to *be* American is to be white. When racial minorities complain about the *slurs* of a public figure like Paula Deen or a *prank* like the TV station airing fake names of the pilots in the Asiana Airlines crash (Wi Tu Lo), they are often told by whites to stop being so sensitive or to take the context of *tradition* or *humor* into account. The ability to dismiss and minimize people of color for being oversensitive is itself one of the privileges that whiteness confers. The broader privilege whites gain from occupying the omniscient vantage point in media and civic life usually goes unnamed.

After George Zimmerman was acquitted of the killing of Trayvon Martin, I wrote a column for *Time* about white privilege. If there was one good thing to come out of that entire tragedy, I said, it was that more white people than ever were expressing solidarity with Martin without pretending that they "were" in any meaningful sense Trayvon Martin. In fact, what prompted my piece was the emergence of a Tumblr site where whites were declaring, "I Am *Not* Trayvon Martin"—that is, they had come to recognize the simple privilege that being white afforded them, the privilege of being categorically exempt from the crime of walking with hoodie.

Many of the thousands of online comments and tweets that followed my piece were a vivid picture of early twenty-first-century white anxiety, if not grievance. The tenor of many was this: *Me, privileged? I work hard/I'm struggling/I've earned everything I have.* That was an understandable set of reactions, if somewhat blinkered for not considering that one could be simultaneously a stand-up guy (or hard-luck case) *and* part of an in-group that pays no social tax on pigmentation.

More interesting were the variations on another theme: *A nonwhite guy who worked in the White House is saying that* white *people have privilege?* Or: *George Zimmerman was Hispanic, and you're Asian, so what the hell are you talking about?* Or, simply: *What right do you, a Chinese, have to talk about white privilege?* The theme here was who has standing. Who has standing to say that white people are privileged? Who has standing to speak and be heard at all on race (or on anything)?

So much of the fervid online debate was unbreakably binary. One was either "beyond race" or a "race baiter." One was either defending white people or attacking them. Zimmerman was either a thug or a victim. Martin too. All of which led me to wonder: In an America where race is still so bifurcated, still so often reduced to black/nonblack, or white/nonwhite, how am I to be understood? As an honorary white? Honorary black? What about the actual honor of simply being seen?

2. Scripts

What makes a culture?
Patterns.
What makes a pattern?
Habit.
What makes a habit?
Choice, repeated.

In 1989 literature professor E. D. Hirsch published a slim book called *Cultural Literacy*, which asserted that success in this society requires command of a prodigious amount of "background knowledge"—tens of thousands of concepts, legends, literary references, historical facts, sayings, scientific terms, social schema—asserting further that too many Americans were illiterate in this national culture. The book's appendix, which ended up drawing far more attention than the scholarly argument that preceded it, was a list of five thousand essential cultural references. The list, claiming to contain "what every American should know," was instead seen as a kind of litmus test: If you don't know these things, you are not really American. Arguments ensued.

These were the years when the "culture wars" really got their name, when a great debate took place in America about whether the work of so-called Dead White Men should be recognized and taught as core to the country's history, literature, and identity. That debate is of course still with us. But in the intervening decades something has shifted: the culture.

Hirsch was called a neoconservative, a Eurocentrist, an elitist, even a racist. But he remained adamant that as much as multiculturalism was to be admired, there needed first to be a firm foundation in a single common culture. Hirsch, we can see now, was right in one important way and wrong in another. He was right to claim that background knowledge matters. Its civic-commercial-ideological vocabulary confers social, economic, and political advantage. It is power. One of the book's best passages quotes the radical Black Panther platform of 1972, filled with allusions to the Declaration of Independence and mimicking the structure of early American jeremiads. The point: conservative forms need not preclude radical content; indeed, radical content becomes far more potent when delivered in conservative forms.

Hirsch was wrong, though, to imply that multiculturalism and a single common culture were at odds. In America, what has happened in the last two decades is that we have come to see—we have chosen to see—that multiculturalism *is* our single common culture. Understanding why Muslims worship the way they do, how Chinese people think about elders, what threads of African custom made it into African American folkways: these are not anthropological curiosities for a white observer to consider. They are the vivid particulars that reveal what is universal about American life and culture—namely, its ability to synthesize cultures from around the world and generate strange, unwieldy, inelegant, beautiful combinations.

Of course, the soil here is very English—the language, traditions of law, social organization, and frames of intellectual and artistic reference that come from England. But then, the soil is also very African—the way the brutality of slavery and the resilience of slaves bent and annealed every fact of life here, from the wording of the Constitution to the cadence of our speech to the forms of our faith and anxiety of our moralism. And whatever else was originally in that soil, its fruit have transcended those origins. America grows stuff that never grew in England or Africa. We are what Albert Murray, who, like Ralph Ellison, played the blues in his music and his writing, called Omni-Americans.

Perhaps Hirsch came to realize this. Not long after his book came out, he published the first of several editions of a *Dictionary of Cultural Literacy*. What's striking about the most recent, from 2002, is how multicultural, how *omnicultural*, it is. Where the 1989 list had nothing to say about Islam, the 2002 dictionary goes on at length about Ramadan and other Muslim rituals. Where the 1989 list mentioned China but not Chinese Americans, the 2002 dictionary includes an entry on the Chinese Exclusion Act. It's striking, too, and fitting, that the 2002 dictionary is the last edition published. We've moved on. The tempo of meme creation and destruction has become too fast for one person to record. The age of Diderot and his encyclopedia or Hirsch and his dictionary yields to the age of us and our Wikis.

In the beautiful, chaotic, stream-of-consciousness sprawl of his Depression-era trilogy *U.S.A.*, John dos Passos includes, over a span of 1,240 pages, two mentions of Chinese people. An unnamed "chinaman" (de-capitalized just so) who speaks with a British accent appears for a few pages as the chauffeur. And there's this, from one of the "Camera Eye" dream-like interstitials:

> where is she going the plain girl in a red hat running up the subway steps and the cop joking the other cop across the street?   and the smack of a kiss from two shadows under the stoop of the brownstone house and the grouchy faces at the streetcorner suddenly gaping black with yells at the thud of a blow a whistle scampering feet   the event?
>
> tonight now
>
> but instead you find yourself (if self is the bellyaching malingerer so often the companion of aimless walks) the jobhunt forgotten   neglected the bulletinboard where the futures are scrawled in chalk
>
> among the nibbling chinamen at the Thalia
>
> ears dazed by the crash of alien gongs the chuckle of rattles the piping of incomprehensible flutes the swing and squawk of ununderstandable talk   otherword music antics postures costumes
>
> an unidentified stranger
> destination unknown
> hat pulled down over the   has he any?   face

In the USA in the 1930s, the self was presumed white. And only by chance would that self, stumbling into a joint filled with nibbling chinamen, find himself suddenly a stranger in a strange land, ears dazed. Only then would *he* be the one without face.

How times have changed.

How have times changed?

At the old Yankee Stadium a few musical riffs used to come over the PA system whenever the home team rallied. One was the opening of "Hava Nagila," starting slow and then picking up momentum as the crowd clapped to each frenzied beat. The other was from Herb Alpert and the Tijuana Brass playing "Zorba the Greek." Same lazy start, same *accelerando*. Same Mediterranean vibe. Those slices of in-game sound may have originated with the Yankees and their Noo Yawk Italian-Jewish-Greek fans, but they're now ubiquitous. When you hear them at a game somewhere else in America, right before the cavalry bugler signals "Charge!," you don't think twice. These are all part of the same all-American soundscape.

Which got me wondering: Is there a Chinese tune that could crack the ballpark repertoire? Which made me remember that at Louisiana State University, where the 1958 football team's crafty defense got the nickname "The Chinese Bandits," a fan was inspired to write the following tune:

Chinese Bandits on their way
Listen what Confucius say
Tiger Bandits like to KNOCK
Gonna stop a touchdown
CHOP CHOP!!!

Tradition now holds that whenever the LSU Tigers' defense makes a third-down stop, fans bow in unison, arms extended, and the marching band plays a Chinese-ish pentatonic ditty. Out of some measure of—what? embarrassment? enlightenment? ignorance?—fans no longer sing the words. But the tune is unchanged; the bowing continues.

Like the "tomahawk chop" performed by fans of the Florida Seminoles and Atlanta Braves, the Chinese Bandits bit contains a dose of backhanded respect for the civilization being belittled (*Gosh those Chinese are good at stealing!*). But fundamentally, this ritual, the casual appropriation and distortion of bits of nonwhite cultures, reinforces the whiteness of the default point of view in public life. If I were Irish, I might like the feisty leprechaun who represents Notre Dame. Because if I were Irish, my place in American society would be so beyond dispute that I could happily suffer that relic of Yankee stereotyping and be known always as Fightin'. The Irish got power and have it today. If I were Native American, though, I'd be less happy about Chief Wahoo, the toothy caricature still the logo of the Cleveland Indians, to say nothing of the Redskins NFL franchise in the nation's capital.

Whether the terms of appropriation of a culture's symbols and stereotyped essences offend or honor has to do less with the content of the symbols than with whether that culture's people enjoy civic equality. Native Americans, I bet, would trade all the brave/warrior/chief/tomahawk honorifics for a fair shot at a decent life in this land. And Chinese Americans? We are neither subjugated nor fully integrated. Many of us have more power than ever before—particularly economic power, and the power of educational achievement and example—but many more do not. And some of us in the second generation still don't feel so culturally secure that we would laugh off, let alone embrace with pride, a sports mascot called "The Scrappy Chink" or "The Mining Chinaman."

But who knows? Maybe the third generation—my daughter's generation—will. Maybe one day a beloved Chinese American athlete-hero will go by the moniker "The Chinese Bandit" and have as his signature ditty a sing-songy Chinatune. Maybe the fourth generation will live in an America where stadiums full of non-Chinese fans will clap along with a Chinatune as they root, root, root for the home team, and where the Chinese American fans in attendance will feel not strange, not masquerading, neither invisible nor conspicuous, but right at home. Maybe we will think of that as progress.

The Jews, writes Neal Gabler in *An Empire of Their Own,* invented Hollywood. A small group of Jewish immigrants were pathologically motivated to escape their pasts and their outsider status—men like Louis B. Mayer, Harry Cohn, Adolph Zucker, the brothers Jack and Harry Warner. Many came from garment business families but went west to claim a domain exempt from the heartbreak and struggle of the Old World, where they could transcend their fathers' failures, give themselves new Anglicized last names, and create families without histories. They projected, literally and psychologically, all their assimilationist dreams of a perfect America onto the screens that in turn framed everyone else's dreams of a perfect America. And they came to the fore at a freakishly perfect moment, when a few ambitious men truly could mold a medium, an industry, a culture, and a country.

Much is made of the comparison between the Jews and the Chinese in America. Outsiders, middleman minorities, chip on the shoulder, striving to bypass an old-boy establishment. This is the Chua-Rubenfeld thesis. But what, nearly a century after the Jews invented Hollywood, might Chinese Americans today comparably invent?

The golden age of the movie industry was so golden because the industry had democratized just enough that a bunch of sons of tailors and peddlers could build an empire—but not so much that they had a lot of competition. They could lord over American culture. Today the fragmentation of our civic and aesthetic life—the way "community" has come to signify a subgroup more often than the whole—means that no single group of immigrants is likely ever to define the interior lives and experiences of hundreds of millions of Americans. There are too many channels, too many screens for anyone to control the means of reflection.

Consider the apparel industry that the Mayers and Zuckers and Warners left behind. Today thousands of Chinese immigrants still toil in American sweatshops making clothes. Jean Kwok's acclaimed novel *Girl In Translation*, about a teen immigrant who's a star student by day and burdened garment worker by night, brought this reality home to many American readers. Meanwhile, organizers and advocates at places like the Chinese Staff and Workers Association in New York continue to combat the exploitation of garment workers.

At the same time, Chinese Americans like Alexander Wang and Jason Wu now make *fashion*. Their designs become the new must-haves. Chinese Americans like Eva Wang, editor of the uber-stylish *Lucky* magazine and a protégé of *Vogue*'s Anna Wintour, make *taste*. Her choices become the new chic. These were not things that Chinese Americans in my youth were expected to do or expected themselves to do—making fashion and making taste.

But timing is everything. And these days, it's not so easy to be a mogul of fashion and taste. There are a million styles, pinned on a million boards, sketched on a million pads, more than can ever be directed by a few tastemakers. The cacophonous, flattening, global churn of modern pop culture has made dominating this game more difficult than ever. So yes, Chinese

Americans today can enter the culture-making business more readily than ever and even make it to the cultural elite. The cultural elite, though, has become just another noisy niche in an age without empire.

The question is: Is that bad news? The Jews who created Hollywood, writes Gabler, invented a whole new America but, in their fierce determination to assimilate, lost themselves. Perhaps it's not possible anymore for any cohort of newcomers to invent a whole new America. Perhaps it's not necessary anymore for those newcomers to lose themselves.

3. Improvisations

It's tempting to look at the arrival and semi-disappearance of Jeremy Lin as a cautionary tale. A parable about the half-life of hype. It was so beautiful while it lasted. "Linsanity": the national frenzy over a young, skinny, Harvard-educated, Taiwanese American walk-on point guard for the New York Knicks of the NBA who went from barely a benchwarmer to an unstoppable force, a scoring machine whose kid-like heart and gloriously free style of play transformed a group of selfish individuals into a true team, who sparked a magical winning spree, who made New York cynics and weary Knicks fans believe again, whose underdog ascent made every Asian American and especially every American of Chinese descent, whether they had ever watched a basketball game, get teary-eyed not just at his court prowess but at the fact that all over America now people of every color were making yellow masks with Jeremy's face and wearing blue jerseys with LIN on the back, and for the first time in this country someone who looked and lived like them—like me—could be the mythic sports action figure that little kids dreamed of being and becoming.

The whole thing lasted, basically, several weeks. Then the Knicks were at last eliminated, their season over, and instead of retaining Lin at the higher price his agents thought he merited, the front office let him leave. He signed a very rich contract as a free agent with the Houston Rockets. To counter the deflating feeling that this was too far from the bright lights and big stage of Madison Square Garden, people in Lin's circle explained that Houston, where China's Yao Ming had once played, had a rabid Chinese and Chinese American fan base and that this move made great business sense and that Linsanity would have a revival the next season. It didn't. Houston signed another point guard, who displaced Lin as franchise cornerstone. Lin's play, while respectable, was not inspired or outstanding anymore. The same national press that had brought him so high now brought him low. *Overrated. Overpriced. Told ya so.* The chants got in his head. His play deteriorated further. He couldn't sleep. He stopped smiling. He cried. He was benched, his big contract and recent legend now millstones more than milestones.

So yes, it's tempting to think of Jeremy Lin in terms of Icarus and overreach, or as just another in the nameless endless roster of flash-in-the-pan pro athletes. Except for this: this man has the capacity to reflect and to articulate his reflections. He is a man of God, and his Christian devotion certainly feeds these capacities. But so perhaps does his Chinese instinct for self-cultivation and finding a middle way. After his failed first season in Houston, Lin spoke candidly at a religious event about how all the affection and attention of Linsanity had affected its object:

> I felt chained to the world's lofty expectations. . . . I had to ask, would I allow myself to listen to what everyone else said about me? Would I allow myself to be consumed by my performance on the court? To be consumed by my job?

> I based my self-worth on how many points I scored or how many games I started. I based my self-esteem on being the player that everyone else expected me to be. But my identity should never have been based on basketball. And this is when God showed me I needed an identity check.
>
> So what did I have to do? I had to re-prioritize my life. I told myself, I'm no longer going to listen to everyone else's voice. I'm not even going to listen to my own voice anymore. I had to get back to listening to God's voice. I had to get back to being what God made me to be. I had to return to my identity as one of God's children, rather than trying to be "Linsanity," which was an identity created by the world.
>
> So my challenge to you today is this: who are you? What is your identity? In order to know the answer, you have to know what makes you the happiest, or what makes you the most proud of yourself. You have to know what makes you the saddest, or what makes you feel like you're not worth anything. What gives you your self-worth or your feeling of importance?

Other people's expectations. These words have for so long been the defining frame of so many Chinese American lives. What society expects. What parents and aunts and uncles and grandmothers expect. What classmates expect. What the people you are attracted to expect. And not just for achievement but for behavior in general. This is the cage built by Tiger Mothers and their fixed notions of success, by Seth MacFarlane sitcoms that ridicule Chinese characters (with a postmodern self-exculpatory wink), by the child's knowledge of the parents' sacrifices that make every opportunity an obligation, by narratives that deem Chinese men unmanly, by the surprise in the eyes of people who didn't expect someone with these eyes and this hair to speak English/play sports/fill-in-the-blank so well.

Jeremy Lin didn't on this occasion address the larger frame of societal expectations. He spoke about one man's confusion—about how the public's insatiable appetite for Linsanity, for an endless upward spiral of performance and for him to represent rather than to be, leached every ounce of intrinsic motivation from his play and his life. He named his failure and examined it. He invited others to behold it. And because he is able to do this, it turns out his story really *can* be a parable—not of failing to live up to expectations but of failing to live unconfined by them.

This parable, which is perhaps less Hollywood than his original story, doesn't require that Lin now become a superstar. He's not a headline-generating player anymore, although he doesn't exactly sit at the end of the bench either. That's all right. He is now showing others, with an open heart and an uncertain sense of where things will go next, how to transcend the limits of another game.

CHARACTER GAME:
WHEN I ________, I AM ACTING CHINESE.
WHEN I ________, I AM ACTING AMERICAN.

Saul Bellow and Philip Roth chronicled the twentieth-century assimilation of Jews, and they did so in a way, with a Jewish sensibility and Jewish voice and Jewish humor, that in the end made *America's* sensibility more Jewish. For their part, Chinese American artists today tell a different kind of story: not of assimilation but something else. "Assimilation" is a word from a passing age; it meant trying to fit in with the white people who dominated the territory. Today's challenge is claiming and renaming the territory. It's showing there are many more ways now to be Chinese American and therefore American.

One path is to be like Bill Cheng and just claim stuff people didn't think you could ever claim. Cheng is author of *Southern Cross the Dog*, a novel of the American South set in the Negro quarter of a small town in Mississippi after the 1927 flood. Cheng, a recent MFA from Hunter College, lives in Brooklyn and has never set foot in the South. He is young, and his soft face and fuzzy hair make him look not yet fully awake, or even fully formed. Yet his command of Delta cadence, his painterly eye, his feel for the structure of myth have dazzled some of the best novelists in America.

A few critics mistrusted the dazzle. Was this an audacious feat of imagination, they wondered, or a merely creditable act of impersonation? Was this an authentic voice, or was it ventriloquism? (When is a novel *not* an act of ventriloquism?) Cheng doesn't appear to care. He's just writing his passion, which is not Chinese in subject matter or style or implication. He's telling a great story about a time and place that captured his imagination. His path is to defy expectation of role/voice/slot/topic.

Another path is to be like Gish Jen and to happily write about being Chinese American, exploring the meaning and absurdity of acculturation and self-reinvention in acclaimed novels like *Mona in the Promised Land* and *Typical American* and in a recent set of essays about craft across East-West borderlines called *Tiger Writing*—works layered with wit and compassion for forgivable hypocrisies and the lies we tell ourselves. Jen is conscious of lineages, from her father's father's father on down to her children's imagined children. Her path is to map these lineages, to limn the meaning of Chinese American identity with unflinching eyes and an open heart.

Another path is to inject a very Chinese way into topics that seem to have nothing to do with Chineseness, as the director Ang Lee has done in each of his ambitiously divergent films. *Sense and Sensibility*, *Brokeback Mountain*, *The Life of Pi.* Their subjects, plots, and settings are widely varied; what they have in common is that they explore a preoccupation of this Taiwan-born artist, whose choice to make movies discomfited his parents well into *his* fifties: the conflict of obligation and desire; the malleability of self-story to fit what a culture wants or needs to hear and see; the illusion of individual control or autonomy. Lee has observed that this preoccupation is very Chinese but also that the Chineseness of his artistic obsession and method isn't intentional or even conscious. It's simply the irresistible consequence of *being him*.

Another path is to displace all the tension and contradiction of being Chinese American into directly allegorical form, as Charles Yu does in his novel *How to Live Safely in a Science Fictional Universe.* This is a book about a time-travel engineer, named Charles Yu, who lives in a bubble out of time, avoiding conflict, halfheartedly searching for a father who disappeared but who bequeathed the very technology that makes time travel possible. Neither the character Charles Yu nor the author Charles Yu says much about being a son of immigrants. Neither one has to.

Another path is to embody in deed and word what happens when you take every model-minority stereotype and fearlessly invert, subvert, convert it into something awesome. This is Eddie Huang, the brash restaurateur and food-show host on Vice TV. His memoir *Fresh Off the Boat* chronicles how he grew up the son of Taiwanese immigrants living against type, playing football and smoking pot and idolizing Tupac. He tried being a lawyer. He tried being a stand-up comic. He tried every way of shadowboxing with expectation until, at age thirty, he came back home to what was always there: food and his love of taking Chinese cuisine and making remixes, with soul food or Caribbean food or French food or whatever else came into his kitchen. His famed restaurant, Baohaus in the East Village, was one result of this journey. His voice—profane, slangy, spicy, hip-hop, Chinese, casual, intense, throwing down, *winging it*—was the other.

Still another path, of course, is to see all these paths as the same path—all leading to a greater knowledge of self and a deeper knowledge that we have more in common than we think. This path assimilates paths into one another. Talk about a Chinese sensibility. (Talk about an American sensibility.)

From *Improvisation for the Theater*, by Viola Spolin:

> *Avoiding the How*
>
> It must be clear in everybody's mind from the very first workshop session that How a problem is solved must grow out of the stage relationships, as in a game. It must happen at the actual moment of stage life (Right now!) and not through any pre-planning. Pre-planning how to do something throws the players into "performance" and/or playwriting, making the development of improvisers impossible and preventing the player in the formal theater from spontaneous stage behavior.
>
> In almost every case a student new in the theater workshops thinks performance is expected.

From *Jazz Cliché Capers*, by Eddie Harris:

> After about twelve years of copying the top twenty guys on your particular instrument, you should be able to construct your own ideas of a constructive solo. A musician who solos who has not copied from recordings of other artists may find himself soloing just like a certain recording artist without knowing it. The funny thing about it is the copier thinks he's the original player of this style.
>
> I think you should copy the solos from each record—note for note; by this I mean the "so-called mistakes" also. The "so-called mistakes" the artist made on the record are things I think you should also do—reason being that many times a soloist meant to do something that you thought might have been a mistake.

When I was in high school, having played the violin since fourth grade, I discovered two ways to branch out from the cliché of the excellent Chinese classical violinist. First, my friend Rob Gutowski and I would go to the band room after school and jam. Rob played piano. We'd listened to a ton of Keith Jarrett. Inspired by the epic live improvised concerts Jarrett and his band recorded in the 1970s, we made up mélanges of tonal and atonal, free jazz and modern classical. We had no idea where our "pieces" were going. We just listened intently to each other. Occasionally we had an audience, but mostly it was the two of us in almost a trance state. Those sessions shaped me deeply. They were a respite from all the little ways that, as a Chinese kid in a white school and town, I was always performing.

The other thing I did around that time was try my hand at writing music. I was an aficionado of the Baroque period. Vivaldi was by far my favorite, but I became familiar with the whole ecosystem of composers surrounding Vivaldi in time and in geography, from Corelli and Scarlatti and Geminiani to Telemann and Bach and Handel. I listened to the records, eagerly checking them out of the library or ordering them from Record World using the thick Schwann's catalog of recordings. Whenever I went to New York City, I went to Patelson's classical sheet-music store near Carnegie Hall and bought the complete scores of my favorite concertos. I internalized the patterns, knew who had influenced whom. It got to where all I needed to hear was four or five seconds of a Baroque piece, and I could tell you who the composer was. I could whistle a phrase by one and make up my own ending to it in the style of another. Soon I started to compose short sonatas, then a concerto, eventually a full choral work. The pieces were a pastiche of other people's patterns, mainly Vivaldi and Bach. Because I hadn't learned formal music theory except what I had absorbed from all my score reading, the pieces were not that sophisticated. But they were mine. This was a time when my parents might have preferred I devote energy to mastering the sounds and lineages of Chinese. I had little interest in that. It was also a time, though, when I had a desire *not* to listen to Top 40 or '70s rock, as everyone else my age was doing. I carved out my own kind of assimilation: assimilating not to the pop culture of that moment but to the music of an era of my own choosing. I lost myself in time and history. I began to make my self.

4. Performers

Susan Cain's book *Quiet*, a "manifesto for introversion," as she puts it, describes the moment when the extrovert became the preferred American personality type. It was the early twentieth century, when consumer capitalism was about to become the dominant form of interpersonal interaction in the United

States, when Dale Carnegie transformed salesmanship from a skill to a way of being. Cain, citing the cultural historian Warren Susman, describes this as the transition from a "culture of character" in the nineteenth century to a "culture of personality." In the culture of character, Americans cared about duty, citizenship, honor, manners, golden deeds. In the culture of personality, people want to be magnetic, forceful, energetic, fascinating. Everyone becomes a charmer. Everyone's in the marketplace all the time. Before long, leadership gurus are urging everyone to sell "The Brand of You."

This selling, this narcissism, this constant impression-management has made our culture solipsistic to the point of a black-hole-like collapse. (And this was even before Facebook.) Such an environment doesn't reward people who, by upbringing or temperament or both, are more likely to downplay individual specialness and deflect individual credit. Which is perhaps why so many Chinese Americans (and other Asian Americans) feel they should sign up for assertiveness training in contemporary corporate America. But Cain's argument is that introversion is not a defect; it is a virtue—and that America's whole way of being is dramatically out of balance. She is right.

This moment, of a great economic reset and a recalibration of America's once unipolar power in the world, may be yielding a new yearning: to stop selling all the time. To release the illusion of control or mastery of our environment. To live a more purpose-driven and relationship-minded life. To swing back toward a culture of character. What will keep America from disintegrating into 317 million salespeople with no customers and no citizens is learning to appreciate quiet cultivation of virtue, to attend anew to manners and golden deeds, to act more with responsibilities and duties in mind, to move with more awareness of both inheritance and legacy.

In short, to become a little more Chinese.

Now, to be sure, there's plenty about Chinese culture that prioritizes facades over the real, and values extrinsic reward and prestige over intrinsic motivation and worth. Also, plenty about Chinese culture that is aggressive and decidedly not shy or reflective. Just walk through a street market in Shanghai or Flushing. What Chinese culture at its best can and should bring, however, is a cultivation of a notion of self that is not divorced from others—that is, in fact, defined by relationship with others. What Chinese culture at its best can bring to America is a better balance between being an individual and being in a community. A healthier hybrid.

Spend a day in Las Vegas with Tony Hsieh, and you can envision what such a hybrid could be like. The Zappos founder and CEO recently moved his online retail company to downtown Vegas, and he's invested massively in revitalizing this civic desert. Here, all mashed up, is the electricity of a neighborhood-scale start-up, deep attention to cultivating community, obsession with metrics yet deference to the intangible magic of art and human relationships, and an earnest, even cultish devotion to the higher purpose of Delivering Happiness (the title of his memoir and slogan of his company). Hsieh embodies the hybrid: he's an American gambler with a Chinese long view; he is supremely confident yet mainly silent; he has so little of the American need to sell himself, so little extroversion, that he jokes even his friends aren't sure he likes them. The Tony Hsiehs of our time, CEOs or not, have something uniquely compelling to offer: an example.

Is America ready to receive this offering? Is America ready to let Americans of Chinese ancestry be this way and succeed, rather than forcing them to mimic the performances of a Dale Carnegie or his imitators? The question is all wrong. There is no America that "lets" and "receives" anymore. There is only the America we decide to make. We are making it now, Americans Chinese and not Chinese. We are spreading new norms and styles, weaving new ways of succeeding, elevating the value of quiet. If this isn't exactly a manifesto for introversion, it's at least a call for a wiser way to show what this country can make of the world. Listen for it.

Hi, everybody. . . . So, I'm Irish.

There aren't a lot of Chinese American stand-up comedians. Joe Wong may be the best known. This slight, bespectacled, forty-something scientist emigrated from China in 1994 to attend Rice University in Texas and got a PhD in biochemistry. Along the way he decided to try his hand at comedy. He took adult education classes, was unafraid to fail, and started going to open mikes. A researcher by day, he's had an improbable ascent as a comic, from small clubs in Houston and Boston to the *Ellen DeGeneres Show* to Letterman. In 2010 he headlined the Radio and TV Correspondents' Dinner, performing for Vice President Biden. In 2012 he won the Great American Comedy Festival.

Now we have a president who's half-black, half-white, and this gives me a lot of hope. Because I'm half not-black, half not-white. [beat] Two negatives make a positive.

While his jokes are good on paper, it's Wong's slow, deadpan delivery that kills. He isn't too eager to please. He lets things sink in. His accent, slightly halting pace, and unconventional emphasis of certain rhythms make it hard not to keep listening and hard not to root for him. Of course, I naturally would say that: Joe Wong reminds me of Chinese dads I know, including my own. But to see largely white audiences laugh with him confirms it. His talent *translates.*

> *Recently my son came home and just said to me, "Hey Dad, am I white," and I was like, "Oh no, you're not white, you're yellow," and he looked at his arm and he was like, "Hey Dad, this doesn't look yellow to me." I said, "Well, it's not exactly yellow, but in this country, everybody has to have a color, and that's the color they give us."*

My dad didn't tell a lot of prefabricated jokes, but he had a great sense of humor, and we spoke often in the kitchen about "Chinese humor"—his and in general. What is Chinese humor? The question evokes Justice Potter Stewart's definition of obscenity: you know it when you see it. But there's surely something more effable. It's about absurdity. It's underdog humor. It's a touch dark. It's about characters thinking they're bigger and more important than they truly are. OK, this describes everything from Mel Brooks to Chris Rock. But Chinese humor is particularly about misplaced face, about social misunderstandings or misalignments. It's more about the gap between official appearances and reality. It's why my dad's favorite comedian in America was Rodney Dangerfield, with his shoulder-wiggling, tie-straightening tagline: "No respect!" Come to think of it, maybe that was Chinese *American* humor.

> *I grew up in China. Who didn't?*

When Joe Wong tried recently to bring his stand-up act back to his native China, it didn't quite work. His jokes about parallel parking and mistaken racial identities fell flat with Chinese audiences. Setups that were natural in America, where audiences knew to *wait for it*, provoked premature reactions in China. He adjusted, like any pro does, and found topics that could truly cross cultures. But he didn't keep the experiment going. He came home to do more shows. To work the circuit. To develop more material for audiences that will get the joke even before he opens his mouth.

> *After I graduated from Rice University, I decided to stay in the United States—because in China I can't do the thing I do best here: being ethnic.*

The *New York Times* online recently produced an engrossing video called *Standing Out in Chinatown*. It lasts three and a half minutes, with a hip soundtrack and no narration. First the camera scans streets and markets crowded with casually dressed people who look like my Po Po, my mother's mother, and her caregiver, Li Tai Tai. Then we hear from a series of random individuals: a graphic designer, a neighborhood lady, a fashion writer, a hairstylist. They are all ethnic Chinese. Men and women, immigrants and ABCs, old and young. Some speak English, some Mandarin. Each talks about his or her fashion choices that day—their personal principles of style and public self-presentation. "A combination of vintage and a little bit of unusualness." "A little bit British style." "A little crazy." As they speak, the camera zooms in on their shoes and belts and skirts and accessories.

I don't often go back to the corner of South Street and Clinton Street, the corner in Manhattan where my Po Po lived the last twenty years of her life. But when I walk through this or any other Chinatown in America, what I see now is more colorful, more unpredictable, more modish than what I remember. Maybe they've always been there, these secret fashionistas, private people making well-considered choices to look a certain way in public and paying attention to what others are wearing. Performers, all. Or maybe something new is going on, a bloom of a thousand trends that departs from the ways of the old-timers yet pays a certain homage as well.

This fusion of aesthetics past and present can be felt in the recent renovations of two iconic museums: the Museum of Chinese in America, or MOCA, in New York's lower East Side, and the Wing Luke Museum in Seattle's Chinatown/International District. MOCA has been around since 1980 but in 2009 moved into an elegant, timber-and-concrete space designed by Maya Lin. The Wing, as its new marketing materials call it, was named after Seattle's first Asian American city councilman, and in 2008 it relocated from an old garage to a gloriously refurbished, brick, single-room-occupancy hotel. It now stands as one of the country's preeminent curators of pan-ethnic Asian Pacific American history. Walking through these two modernized museums are tourists and schoolchildren of every kind; walking by them each day are people of Chinatown: pensioners, peddlers, speakers of many dialects. It's easy to think of these people as stuck in time. They are not. They're making their way, like the other Americans all around them.

When, near the turn of the twenty-first century, a teenager named Wei Chen emigrated with his father from China, he had reason to believe in the dream of American identity: he had arrived in Philadelphia, city of brotherly love, capital of the Revolution. But at South Philadelphia High School he quickly found himself in a sulfurous purgatory of urban poverty and violence. Black students were bullying and terrorizing Asian students. They chased them. They taunted them. They beat them. The teachers were passive, and the principal ignored it. It got so bad that Wei Chen and other Asian students were scared to do the very thing their parents had brought them here to do: get an American education. Except Wei Chen did get an American education. He was schooled in the legacy of color-coded resentment and how life in an American city can make categories like "Citizen" and "Alien" and "Native" and "Non-Alien" seem like niceties. In those South Philly hallways there were just two categories: in and out. Wei Chen was most definitely out.

After months of this daily terror, though, he finally reached his limit. What he did next came partly from an immigrant's instinct of how to improvise power from powerlessness. But it came also from his close study of the tactics and history of the American civil rights movement. He began to keep a little notebook, documenting every incident of bullying. He asked for the name and contact information of every other kid who was getting bullied. He organized them into a Chinese Students Association. He won their trust. Before long, at Chen's direction, against the wishes of many of their parents, dozens of Chinese students at South Philadelphia High School stopped going to school. They boycotted.

They also filed a civil rights complaint. Chen and his compatriots refused to make the complaint about their tormentors—

refused to frame this as a race war. Instead they directed their complaint against the principal and district leaders who had failed to create an environment of safety and learning for *all* students. They went to the local press. The story got picked up. And after a wave of national media attention, the principal was fired, and a chastened district changed its practices.

When I spoke with Chen a few years after he'd graduated from South Philly High, he was working odd jobs to save money for community college. But he was also spending many unpaid hours as a teacher. He teaches other Chinese and Asian students how to organize, how to advocate. He mentors other immigrant kids in situations of conflict or looming violence how to keep up hope and how to foster a spirit of nonviolence. He shares the lessons he absorbed from his experience at South Philly High. Wei Chen, in short, teaches citizenship. He didn't set out to do this. It's simply how life in this country called him to act.

Gish Jen writes:

> All of this feeling my way forward led eventually to the novelist I am today—the one I described earlier as concerned with private experience, with questions of love and friendship and family and purpose, but also to a perhaps unusual degree with context-oriented questions like, What doors are open, and what doors are closed? And, Whose house is this? And, What is the way? Questions that—because I have asked them of the American context—have, despite their Chinese origin, ironically rendered me a distinctly American writer.

The subtitle of Jen's wise, nuanced book *Tiger Writing* is *Art, Culture, and the Interdependent Self.* She explores, in three essays about her father, family, and formation, this interplay between independent and interdependent selves, Western and Eastern, American and Chinese. Between public voice and private identity. Between the idea that such binaries matter and the idea that they don't.

My friend Cheryl Chow died in 2013 of brain cancer at age sixty-six. She was the third of five children and the only daughter of a great matriarch, Ruby Chow, a restaurateur who had presided unofficially over Seattle's Chinatown and was a pioneering politician—the first Asian American to serve on the King County Council. At a glance, it might seem the daughter followed the path of the mother. Like Ruby, Cheryl was tough and no-nonsense, with a blunt conversational style that social psychologists call "low-elaborative." Like Ruby, Cheryl became an effective politician, serving on the Seattle City Council and the Seattle School Board. Throughout, Cheryl devoted herself to the Seattle Chinese Community Girls Drill Team, which her mother had founded decades earlier.

But a closer look at Cheryl Chow's life reveals a path all her own. She became a teacher and a principal in the Seattle School District. She was active in the Girl Scouts. She became a mentor and a champion of mentoring. She coached basketball for decades through Seattle Parks and Rec. And she fell in love with Sarah. All her life, Cheryl knew she was gay. All her life she acted as if she weren't. She dated men. She never explored this aspect of her private self—not in public, certainly, but not in private either, even with her mother. Especially with her mother. Not until deep into adulthood did Cheryl enter into a relationship with a woman—Sarah, an educator too, whose young daughter called Cheryl "Kai-Ma," Cantonese for "godmother," but eventually thought of her as simply another mother. And not until Cheryl had developed central nervous system lymphoma, and the cancer had become far advanced, requiring aggressive treatment, did she come out and make public her decade-long relationship with Sarah.

She did so at the sixtieth anniversary celebration of the Seattle Chinese Community Girls Drill Team in 2012. "I said, 'What the hell,'" Cheryl told a *Seattle Times* reporter. "I said, 'Well, I can say anything I want now.'" In what turned out to be the final months of her life, she became a new kind of advocate, with more power and inspirational force than she'd ever wielded in public office. She told young people to feel comfortable talking about being gay. She championed marriage equality (which Washington State approved that year by referendum). She adopted Sarah's daughter. She married Sarah. Thirteen days later, she died.

Sometimes I reflect on the path Cheryl followed and the one she created. Her many lives—the many chambers of identity she inherited and expanded and knocked down and remade—leave me wondering, of her and of us all: *What doors are open? Whose house is this? What is the way?* Cheryl Chow's life teaches us: All doors are open. This is everyone's house. We are the way.

Fidelity, Or, the Impossibility of Translating a Poem

Here is one of the greatest poems ever penned in Chinese—"Mountain Holiday, Thinking of My Brothers in Shandong," by Wang Wei:

> 王维的《九月九日忆山东兄弟》
> 独在异乡为异客，
> 每逢佳节倍思亲。
> 遥知兄弟登高处，
> 遍插茱萸少一人。

Here is the pinyin transliteration, which conveys the sound and rhythm of the original:

> *dú zài yì xiāng wéi yì kè,*
> *měi féng jiā jié bèi sī qīn.*
> *yáo zhī xiōng di dēng gāo chù,*
> *biàn chā zhū yú shǎo yì rén.*

Here is a fine translation, which doesn't conform to the line structure or music of the original but captures its essence artfully:

All alone in a foreign land,
I am twice as homesick on this day
When brothers carry dogwood up the mountain,
Each of them a branch—and my branch missing.

Here is a word-for-word translation, which is more faithful to the impressionism of Chinese but leaves the reader with a false sense that the original was inelegant:

Alone in foreign land being foreign guest
Every facing holiday twice think relatives
Far know brothers climb high place
Everyone places dogwood less one person.

Here is another, faithful not to the original content or to rules of Chinese poetry but to the feeling the original evoked in me when I first encountered it:

In the land of my birth
Not alone but homesick still
When uncles send images from their latest travels,
Each of them smiling—and one brother missing.

Here is another, faithful to the feeling that the original can evoke in anyone:

All alone in a foreign land.

CHAPTER 7

Father Tongue

1.

There is a "vocabulary gap" between poor children and other children that opens up at an early age and is both a consequence and a cause of inequality. By age three, according to the Harvard Center on the Developing Child, kids from low-income families have only half the vocabulary of their higher-income counterparts. Advantage and disadvantage compound, across generations. This is especially so if the low-income child or her family doesn't speak English as a first language.

There is a different but comparable vocabulary gap for children in households where two languages are spoken but one is utterly dominant. Those early differences in uptake of the languages also quickly compound. The dominant language becomes more dominant in the child's verbal life, and the secondary atrophies. This is a third-generation gap.

The first real word my daughter, Olivia, spoke was "tongue." She pronounced it "dahng" with a flat *a* and her tongue way back in her mouth. She was six months old. It vibrates in my memory like the gong of a bell. I recall how surprised and bemused her mother, Carroll, and I were at this improbable, oddly apt first word.

In fairly short order, Olivia became a little sense-making machine, picking up words at a rapid clip. By the time she was twenty months old, she could say hundreds of words. They're all listed neatly in a journal that her nanny, Melissa, kept. They're all English words. I tried from the start to speak Chinese to Olivia, but it usually happened like this: we'd be playing on the floor, and I'd be naming and saying things in the exaggerated, elongated phrasings of "parentese," as child psychologist Alison Gopnik calls it—"What's thiiiiis? Yes it *is* a cat!"—when suddenly I'd remember to say something in Chinese. So I'd point to something else, like her feet or her tummy, and name it in Chinese. When she got slightly older, I'd ask a question like, *Ni de duzi zai nali?* ("Where's your tummy?"). She would point to her little tummy. So she understood. But I didn't ask her to repeat after me. I realize now that what little Chinese I was teaching her, I was teaching in the way of English speakers: noun-heavy, verb-light, classifying objects rather than illuminating interrelationships.

2.

There are words and figures of speech in any language that native speakers never think to excavate. In English, when someone is "whipsawed," we simply think of that person being caught between two difficult situations. We don't envision the operation of a narrow crosscut saw. In Chinese, I grew up hearing *mashang* as a single concept: "immediately" or "urgently." It didn't occur to me till years later that it means "up on the horse." Same with *shengqi*, which in my integrated Chinese-English conceptual brain simply meant "get mad" but in fact is "generate steam."

Nor did I ever realize that *luanqibazao*—"chaotic"—was a construction ingeniously conceived to represent chaos, in which the words for chaos (*luan*) and misfortune (*zao*) were interrupted, for no good reason, by the words for seven (*qi*) and eight (*ba*). There's a similar expression from British English, "to be at sixes and sevens," with the same meaning of disarray. But whereas that idiom derives from dice and games of hazard, the Chinese version comes from a broader semantic tradition, as Perry Link describes, in which numbers are frequently inserted into phrases to give them color and four syllables, and thus more emphasis. So *luanqibazao* is more dire a form of chaos than simply *luan* or *luanzao.* And *yiqingerchu*—"crystal clear," or "one clear two neat"—is more emphatic than simply *qingchu.* These things, so fascinating to me now, were not things I used to notice. To break down what you had taken for granted is not something most people do until forced.

Numbers were, of course, some of the first words Olivia learned to say in Chinese. She was probably able to count to ten—*yi, er, san, si, wu, liu, qi, ba, jiu, shi*—by the time she had several hundred English words. These were probably also among the first characters she learned to write. During her early years, when Carroll and I both became so busy in our work, frenetic in our ambitions, silent about our stresses, I too came to say those words again, slowly and to myself, and to visualize the ideographs as a way of recentering. Ten deep breaths, eyes closed. All I let into my mind during each inhalation and exhalation was the image of a single character.

3.

> Once they marry, Chinese Americans tend to stay married—with a divorce rate less than half that of the general population (4.4 percent vs. 10 percent).
>
> —*Portrait of Chinese Americans,* University of Maryland, 2008

Sometimes, though not as often anymore, friends I haven't seen in years will ask after my daughter. "How's Ming?" they'll say. "She's great," I'll reply, "but she's not Ming anymore. She's Olivia again."

For over a year, when Olivia was seven turning eight, she chose to go by her Chinese name, Ming. From infancy, her strength of will had been apparent. But I was surprised nonetheless when one day she informed her second-grade teacher matter-of-factly that she would henceforth answer only to Ming. She crossed out "Olivia" from her nameplate at school. She'd already learned to write "Liu Ming" in Chinese (劉明), and now she signed all her homework "Ming" and added the ideographs. She let all her friends know to call her by her new name. She let her mother know, and her grandparents. At first they all hesitated; eventually they all obeyed.

The people asking after Ming now are usually smiling, because they remember how serious Olivia was about it all; there was something amusing and impressive about this little person's act of self-determination. And I am usually smiling as well, because I remember so fondly that time of my life.

That is perhaps surprising. Olivia became Ming as spring became summer in 2006. It was the start of my second full year of single fatherhood, months after my divorce had gone final, less than two years after my wife had told me on Halloween night, in our seventh going on eighth year of marriage, that our marriage had ended.

It was a period of stillness and lingering smoke after a great fire. Even with shoots arising amid the ashes—I had recently begun a new relationship—I was often sad. My time with Olivia was a respite, but I didn't want her to sense that too much. I was protective of her and, in her indirect way, she of me. We set out earnestly to create new routines at home. During long summer mornings of imaginary play she initiated games in which we enacted cinematic scenes of threat and loss and rescue.

Parenting alone in divorce is an experience of compression. My daughter was now with me half of each week and every other weekend. There were some responsibilities that were thus cut neatly in two: I made breakfast and packed lunches, got her to and from school or camp, but just on the days Olivia was with me. There were other responsibilities, meanwhile, that in an ideal world would have suffused every day of the week and that now had to be managed in half the time. Responsibilities like teaching my daughter how to be Chinese.

Olivia's mother, Carroll, is, as I noted once when I was rhapsodizing about the hybrid possibilities of our union, Scotch-Irish-Jewish. And our child is indeed a hybrid beauty. But ensuring that Olivia was exposed and connected to her Chinese heritage was my job alone. I signed her up for Chinese classes; I got a daily desk calendar to teach 365 Chinese characters; I spoke more Chinese around the house, weaving words and phrases into everyday chitchat; we found an animated PBS series called *Sagwa*, about a family of cats in ancient China, that she loved; Nai Nai came to visit more frequently, and we went to visit her in DC and eat her home cooking; I myself began to expand my own repertoire of stir fry.

Olivia began to identify with me in small new ways. "I'm Chinese too!" she would proudly declare as we walked through Chinatown in search of dinner. She opened and started using the calligraphy ink and brush set that she'd gotten as a gift two years earlier. She observed that our hands looked alike. The two of us went on cozy camping expeditions (to our backyard). We made up jokes and traditions around the house that still stand. I know little about what her life was like with Carroll then—Ming was not just discreet but compartmentalized. What I do know is that when she was with me, it was as blissful as sadness could possibly be.

One high point of that time was a trip that Ming, Nai Nai, and I took together to China and Taiwan in the spring of 2007. My mom and I had been there multiple times, but this was the first time for my daughter. She soaked up everything, from the decaying grandeur of the Forbidden City to the lilting accent of our tour guide to the Beijing dumpling shop at night to the densely packed riverside hills of Guilin. On her eighth birthday we were to see the Great Wall. I looked out the hotel window when I awoke; it was raining and foggy. I was about to brace Ming for disappointment when she jumped up and said, "Daddy! Guess what? We're going to get to go to the Great Wall *in the rain!*" A Seattle girl. Later, when she got to meet her then-ninety-seven-year-old great-grandmother—her Tai Nai Nai—so that four generations were in a single room, Ming understood how rare and wondrous this was.

When we came back from that trip, everything felt more solid. There was a new sense of safety, of place. I called her not Ming, as her schoolmates did, but Xiao Ming, Little Ming, with the correct tones, the same affectionate diminutive she would hear growing up in a Chinese household. Which, in a third-generation American way, she was.

One afternoon several weeks later, we were sitting in the kitchen nook drawing together. Ming said somewhat casually, "I think I'm not going to be Ming anymore." I tried to play it as cool as I had at the beginning. "Oh yeah? You're ready to go back?" I asked. She continued to draw but peered up slightly to gauge my reaction and, seeing no obvious injury, shrugged. "Mm mm mmm," she murmured, with the offense-minimizing inflection of "I don't know."

Where does tact come from? It comes in part from awareness of pain and the potential of words to cause it. It comes too from a readiness to move beyond denial. We had lived in a little bubble together, had found in our shared Chineseness a shelter of meaning against a storm of change. Now she was ready to go forth. With a shrug that made me ache with gratitude and grief, Ming became Olivia once again. When third grade began and kids greeted her with a cheerful "Hi, Ming!" she patiently corrected them, one by one. And that was that.

We don't really talk about it anymore. Today we are all at a new, and I suppose modern, normal. Carroll and I are amicable co-parents. I met Jená, who is soon to be my wife and Olivia's stepmother and whose daughter, Zoey, nine years older, is Olivia's big stepsister. For Olivia, living in two households has become second nature. Now she's a bit embarrassed about the time—*so long ago*, against the denominator of her fifteen-plus years—when she changed her name. "Remember when you were Ming?" I'll sometimes say. "Yeaaah," she'll answer, a little sheepishly. I want to ask why the sheepishness. I manage to resist.

Over a period of fourteen months, Olivia Liu made plain to the world that she was her own person—and my daughter. This time remains so vivid to me. It was the very definition of bittersweet: a kind of sweetness, not a kind of bitterness. I call it the Year of Ming.

4.

According to the American Council for the Teaching of Foreign Languages, the number of kindergarten through twelfth-grade students in the United States studying Mandarin Chinese rose nearly 200 percent between 2005 and 2008. The number of college Chinese language programs has also more than tripled since 2002. There are no statistics for how many students stay in their program for more than a year, or how many ever attain proficiency.

Those who ignore Chinese school are doomed to repeat it. In Olivia's elementary years, I took her to a Saturday class for a while and then tried out an afterschool class. I would sit in the back of a borrowed third-grade classroom, fitting myself into a little chair as the teacher tried to hold the kids' attention. What was different from the Chinese school of my youth, though, was that about a third of the kids now were not Chinese. They were living proof that more non-Chinese Americans were beginning to wonder, in the words of one program's promotional material, "Will our children be ready to meet—and compete with—the new kids on the block?"

I'm pretty sure "new kids on the block" meant the youth of rising China and not Chinese American kids. But in any event, the anxious competitiveness that's causing the nationwide surge in Chinese language learning was absent from Olivia's classes. What prevailed there was the sober, even dispirited air of kids and parents who were starting to realize just how damned hard it is to learn Mandarin.

As her age crossed double digits, Olivia began to complain that Chinese school was too "kiddy." I had to agree. Because the class had so wide a range of students, from those who'd been hearing Chinese all their lives to those who were meeting Chinese kids for the first time, the teacher lingered on the most basic things like colors and days of the week, using exercises made for preschoolers. So I gave Olivia a choice: either continue going to the weekly class, or have a weekly tutorial at home with me. She thought about it for a moment and said, "OK, you."

So on January 4, 2009, I dug out my college textbooks, and we began a Tuesday afternoon ritual that continues to this day. We sit in our kitchen nook for about an hour. We spend about half the time on spoken Chinese, half on written. I teach her to say words and phrases in basic conversational dialogues. When it comes time for writing, I take a sheet of *bai zhi*—white paper—and make a grid of boxes. I fill out the leftmost column with a dozen characters taken from the dialogues. She then fills out the boxes across each row, writing out nine or ten repetitions.

Sometimes her soccer schedule or my travels mean we skip a week or two. Summers we skip even more. But we've had the same orange folder for her weekly writing sheets for over five years, and it's overstuffed now. The pockets have just about ripped off, and the outside is covered entirely with years' worth of Olivia's doodles. As she got older, she complained that the dialogues and subject matter in the textbooks were stilted and boring. "Who even talks like that?" she'd ask. "*Is this mountain higher or that one? Is this river longer or that one*? Ugh!" So I asked how we could make it more interesting. She came up with an idea. She would devise ridiculous sentences in English, some drawing on inside jokes from school and some pure farce. I would then have to consult my pocket English-Chinese/Chinese-English dictionary to translate the sentence. And then she'd have to learn how to say and write the Chinese version of such sentences as:

Rabbits used to eat rulers in the Stone Age.

Toes are very important in one's life.

Howdy, pardner, my name's Ol' Greasy Sparehands, and I've come to be your sheriff.

My translations were not grammatically perfect, but the entire process was hilarious and we'd often end up on the kitchen floor laughing at what she'd come up with or how it sounded in Chinese. This went on for a couple of months, until perhaps she realized that it made our lessons much longer. Eventually I returned to a modified traditional format, in which our lines were neither absurdities nor banalities but simply useful everyday sentences, things she might be able to say to Nai Nai, like "I'm playing soccer next week" or "I'm going outside with my friends."

For all the hours we've spent doing this, my daughter's Chinese hasn't progressed that much. Her vocabulary and sense of syntax are limited mainly to our exercises; she probably would falter in live extended conversation without me there. But part of the victory is that we are doing this at all. She's in high school now, and a foundation has been laid. Flipping through those dozens of sheets in her folder, I see a steadying of her hand from one year to the next. She now has an instinct for what the proper order of strokes should be when writing a new character (top to bottom, left to right, outside to inside). She now knows when a character "looks right"—not just technically correct but calligraphically pleasing. And even though she doesn't ever want to be heard speaking Mandarin by her friends or even by Nei Nei (her pinyin transliteration of Jená's nickname), her pronunciation of Mandarin—her enunciation of the varying tones—is very good. This is what I've given her: a feel, a fighting chance against those new kids on the block.

5.

The linguistic anthropologist Elaine Chun, in a paper called "Ideologies of Legitimate Mockery," catalogs the elements of a "Mock Asian" accent in elaborate technical detail. Such an accent typically is marked by a set of factors, including:

> 1. Neutralization of the phonemic difference between /r/ and /w/ (*wrong* pronounced as *wong*, *right* pronounced as *white*) . . .
>
> 3. Alveolarization of voiceless interdental fricative 'th' (*thank you* pronounced as *sank you*, *I think so* pronounced as *I sink so*) . . .
>
> 7. Epenthetic 'ee' at the end of a closed word (break-ee, buy-ee, look-ee)

The point of Chun's paper is that not all mockery is created equal. Context, intention, the ethnic and even political standing of the mimic to engage in mimicry—all these go into the subtle calculation of what separates, say, Rush Limbaugh doing a crude on-air ching-chong riff to imitate China's then-president Hu Jintao, from comedian Margaret Cho using a mock Asian accent to tell a joke about her own family. When is mockery not mockery? When it's homage.

I am often mindful of what Olivia hears. She is a child of interracial marriage and divorce, a third-generation Chinese American, a student at a big, diverse public high school. All around her are whorls and eddies of ideas and vocabularies and bits of thought. As a father, I try to give her the right kinds of words.

And what a listener she is: Olivia has a great ear for how people talk. She is a mimic extraordinaire. She picks up on vocal style, on shadings of timbre and tone and what they are meant to signal.

Sometimes this makes it hard to get "solemn" and "stern" with her as a father, because just as I'm about to say something, she will interrupt with an observation—"Oh, getting all serious now!"—which forces me to pause and stifle a smile. And one running joke in our family comes from a 2011 trip to Taiwan we took with Nai Nai and Nei Nei. We were in Taipei one afternoon, and Jená, pointing at the towering 101 Building, said, "You can see it from anywhere!" Except how Jená pronounced it was, in Olivia's exaggerated mock-Chinese, "You cahn see it from anyweahhh!"

Nei Nei is an actor and often involuntarily echoes the accent of the people she's with—so that when she's with my mom, she ends up sometimes sounding like a white person trying to sound like a native Chinese speaker speaking English. Now, whenever Nei Nei does it, whether with Nai Nai or anyone else with a foreign accent, Olivia drops a "You cahn see it from anyweahhh!" Nei Nei then swats her, objecting in mock offense and mock self-defense.

Mockery of mockery of mockery: so fun and so meta. Olivia and some of her pals, one who's part Cherokee and another who's half black, joke about each other's races and stereotype each other in ways that are quick and ironic and that (I'm pretty sure) represent progress. One time, Olivia walked into the girls' bathroom at school and seeing three or four younger Asian students she didn't know, asked without skipping a beat, "What'd I miss?" The other kids never picked up on the joke: that this was an impromptu meeting of the Asian club. Still, sometimes I have to caution her—not so much to keep her from truly offending others but to keep her from forgetting that she remains, at least in part, subject to mockery with an intent to wound. I have to remind her that when a benighted politician or ignorant celebrity makes fun of Chinese people for being Chinese and speaking in a Chinese way, they are making fun of *us*. That people still make fun of people who look like *us* (even though, truth be told, with her freckles and a dyed streak of blonde in her dark brown hair, she and I don't look Chinese in the same way). "Ya, I know," she'll reply, and move on. And I'll remark to myself that sometimes, unwittingly, Olivia says "Ya" instead of "Yeah." Just like her Nai Nai.

6.

In 2013, University of Texas child development expert Su Jeong Kim released findings from a study in which she had been following over four hundred Chinese American families for a decade. In most of the families the parents were immigrants from Hong Kong or southern China, and the children were born in the United States. The study showed that children of so-called tiger parents had lower academic achievement and more depression and social alienation than those of parents considered "supportive" or "easygoing." Kim put it succinctly: "Tiger parenting doesn't produce superior outcomes in kids." At least as interesting, though less noticed in the media, was her finding that among Chinese American parents the tiger style was no more prevalent than among European American parents.

One thing I noticed when I read Amy Chua's *Battle Hymn of the Tiger Mother* is that there is no mention of anyone speaking Chinese. This is ironic. It's evidence of the way that mores and the patterns of a culture can shed the language that was once their host and hop, virus-like, into other tongues. It's also evidence of the extent to which the very idea of "tiger parenting" is, like the fortune cookie, an American concoction that satisfies a taste for what people imagine to be Chineseness.

This is not to say I am a knee-jerk critic of Chua or even entirely of tiger parenting. Chua was both victim and beneficiary of a media-cultural complex that oversimplified her book and may not have ever read it. She came to stand for something—ruthlessly disciplined parenting—at a time when Americans felt themselves going soft, falling behind. The public version of Amy Chua was a made-for-cable-and-Twitter updating of the old model-minority stereotype: now the storyline was "*inside the making of* a model minority," and it had violence (burning of stuffed animals!) and tyranny (hours of enforced violin practice with no meals!) and a little insanity (writing multipage memos to the kid after a recital!) to spice it up.

To be sure, Chua was not merely a passive screen upon which anxious, competitive bourgeois American parents were projecting their fears. She did write and sell the book, after all, and do the deeds she wrote about. But if you read the entire book, and not just the infamous excerpt that flew around the Internet, what you see is this: she came, in the second half, to regret the excesses she'd garishly chronicled in the first half. She came to see the psychic costs to her family. And though she felt compelled to report for her kids an ending of achievement and happiness after an interlude of rebellion, it's possible to read into the ending a whiff of wistfulness, even emptiness. What, after the mad meritocratic race to the top, is the point?

As for tiger parenting itself, well, it's all relative. I know Amy Chua. Amy Chua is an acquaintance of mine. And, folks, I am no Amy Chua. She is singularly intense and off-the-charts driven. Next to her I am a hippie. Yet I am also the closest thing to a tiger parent in my own family circle. Neither my father nor my mother was strict. Neither Olivia's mother nor stepmother is by temperament a taskmaster or brutal enforcer. By comparison to them, I have a strong "old school" streak. I am sometimes judgmental, even harsh, when I think Olivia hasn't been responsible or mature. I am rigid about rules, and I have high expectations for her. I occasionally use shame to motivate. I think too many parents think they are their kids' peers, with destabilizing consequences for everyone.

At the same time, I'm more playful, supportive, and simply present in the life of my daughter than my parents were in mine. In fact, I've structured my work life so that during the half week and alternate weekends when Olivia is with me, I am *around*. I am inclined, by nature and by circumstance, to treat our time together as precious. So if there were a creature from mythology that was half-tiger, half-human—and moreover, was not always sure which half to activate or which half events might rouse from dormancy, that'd be my parenting mascot. It's probably the mascot for many children of immigrants who become parents—maybe for many in my Gen X cohort, regardless of ethnicity. All I know is that from time to time, if I'm pushing her to push herself to learn more and do more, my teenaged daughter will tell me to stop being such an Asian parent. Then we will crack up. And then she will go on doing roughly what I'd hoped she would be doing.

7.

Students of French sometimes find as they are learning nouns that they can develop a gut instinct for whether a noun is masculine or feminine. Beyond the obvious (*la mère* ["the mother"], *le père* ["the father"]), that instinct doesn't emerge from outright associations with masculinity or femininity per se—the word for "war" is feminine (*la guerre*), after all, and the word for "flower" masculine (*le fleur*). It comes from a sense of patterns that grows stronger the bigger the learner's vocabulary is and the more data there is to crunch. Nouns that end with *e* tend to be feminine, for instance, while those ending with *age* tend to be masculine. Of course, almost no student of French is crunching actual data on the gender of new words, or even learning explicit heuristics like the *e/age* guideline. It's just about whether something *feels* or *sounds* right or wrong as feminine or masculine.

Chinese does not have this issue, as it doesn't even have definite articles for nouns. But it does have its own form of gendered meaning. Chinese culture famously, perhaps infamously, defaults to the male. That default is found in figures of speech and even how characters are written. One small example is that when women become distinguished and prominent in their fields, they sometimes earn the title "Mr." In Chinese, the compound word is *xiansheng.* Literally, "first-born," but by convention, "Mister" or, less often, "Teacher." Though this is long-standing practice, it's raising eyebrows now in a China where gender roles are modernizing along with everything else. "Why should a woman be called a man just because she's clever?" one commentator in Beijing asked. "Why does she have to be a man to be respected?" Yet for some of the younger women in China who are now being addressed as *xiansheng*, the issue isn't patriarchy; it's merit. They don't want the title because they don't think they've earned it yet.

One notable thing about the Tiger Mother craze was that it was mainly about Tiger *Mothers*—rarely were fathers of any ethnic background in the foreground. As modern as we all are, parenting in our culture continues to have a default gender: female. (That's particularly so when the parenting style is being criticized.)

What, then, is the right way to be a father? What is the right way to be a fatherless father? What is the right way to be a Chinese American fatherless father? What is the right way to be a second-generation Chinese American fatherless father? What is the right way to be a divorced second-generation Chinese American fatherless father?

I'm pretty sure the answer is something my mother still says to me but that I don't remember my father ever saying: *Try your best.* Or maybe it's something I was told by an astrologer the one time I went to see an astrologer, a couple of years after my divorce and not long after I started dating Jená : *Shift now from strength to flexibility.*

Fatherhood is bound up, of course, with manhood. In stereotypical Chinese culture, men are firm and strict, while women are soft and kind. But in stereotypical American culture, Chinese men are weak and wimpy. So here lurks the danger, if you don't know yourself well, of overcompensating for either or both sets of stereotypes. Fortunately for me, I suppose, those crucible years as a single parent made me know myself better. They made me fuse, on the fly, so-called male and female or Asian and Western or hard and soft styles. I don't mind being perceived by Olivia or anyone as "feminine" in my willingness to listen, to heal rifts, to talk feelings. I don't mind being perceived as masculine in my willingness to confront, to be a hard-ass, to force an issue instead of avoiding it. Each day I feel my way forward about when to be each. I try my best to bend.

8.

The linguists Lauren Hall-Lew and Rebecca Starr studied English usage among Chinese Americans in the Bay Area. They found that "Chinese" ways of speaking are persisting even into the third generation. Consider, for example, L-vocalization ("words like *cold* and *skill* sound like *code* and *skew*"), which for native Chinese speakers results from the absence of a "syllable-final |l| in all forms of Chinese." I can hear many immigrants I know pronouncing *cold* like *code.* What these researchers found are people of the 1.5, second, and third generations also pronouncing it that way. Why doesn't this "nonstandard" pronunciation disappear with the passage of generations, as would be typical? Hall-Lew and Starr hypothesize three reasons: one, the relative ethnic concentration of the newest wave of Chinese immigrants to the Bay Area; two, the increased ease for today's Chinese immigrants of staying in contact with and returning to China or Taiwan; and three, the rising cultural cachet of China and rising social appeal of a stylized FOB ("fresh off the boat") cultural identity. In short, it's becoming ever easier and cooler *not* to lose the accent.

In David Henry Hwang's play *Chinglish*, a white businessman from Ohio named Daniel goes to China in search of new opportunities for his struggling sign-making company. He arrives, and everything quickly gets lost in translation. On one level the play is a comedy of errors about this businessman and the machinations of his Chinese partners, rivals, and seducers. On a level below is a more philosophical story about how the dominant is always eventually subverted, how everything contains its undoing. And how each side across a divide always assumes it is losing. At one point, Daniel's main Chinese contact, a vice minister of culture named Xi, bitterly remarks to herself, in Mandarin, "This is why it's so difficult to get ahead of America. Even when you are strong, you still act like you're weak." Which, of course, is just how Daniel and his country see Xi and her country. At this moment of flux and phase shift in geopolitics and geoculture, each side wants simultaneously to regard and disregard, to be like and be unlike, the other.

My daughter, thus far, has not been affected by this tidal tension or by the "rising cultural cachet of China." She is aware, because her father talks about it all the time, that China is resurgent and that this creates challenge and opportunity for America. But perhaps because her father talks about it all the time, she shows little interest in the topic. She shows even less inclination to start taking style cues from new-wave Chinese immigrants or from people in China. She doesn't speak enough Chinese to make a Chinglish blend of her own, or have enough Chinese friends or neighbors to start adopting FOB fashion. And so her sense of the potential for blending, such as it is, comes more from the people we see crowding into Din Tai Fung, the famous Taipei dumpling house that's opened not one but two branches in the Seattle area and draws a vibrant mix of Chinese, Chinese American, and other American patrons, while a group of white-uniformed Hispanic men make the dumplings. Or it comes from watching *Kung Fu Panda* and the Jackie Chan/Jaden Smith remake of *The Karate Kid*, two films she loves and that were made, as films are now, with an eye to pleasing audiences in China as well as America. There's a sensibility in each movie that reveres a base layer of Chinese tradition but requires a top layer of American iconoclasm. She feels at home with narratives like this. The lines she quotes from *Kung Fu Panda* are usually, with full rocker/slacker intonation, Jack Black's.

9.

There is a table about a third of the way through Jin Li's book *Cultural Foundations of Learning: East and West*. It describes "components and dimensions of European-American and Chinese learning models."

In the European-American column, the table lists such purposes or processes as:

Cultivate mind/understand world
Reach personal goals
Active engagement
Inquiry
Personal insights/creativity
Being the best one can be
Curiosity/interest
Pride for achievement
Disappointment/low self-esteem for failure

In the Chinese column, it lists, correspondingly:

Perfect self morally/socially
Contribute to society
Diligence
Endurance of hardship
Application of knowledge
Unity of knowledge and moral character
Commitment ("establish one's will")
Humility for achievement
Shame/guilt for failure

Li's table can be read as either the distillation of enormous amounts of research across cultures and generations—or a summation of clichés about East, West, and "never the twain shall meet." Li is a professor of education and human development at Brown University, and a nuanced scholar, so the table has authority of the first kind. But given the way big ideas trickle down, it's not hard to envision someone well-meaning and less nuanced, at some conference years hence, showing a PowerPoint version of this table to describe the differences between white and Chinese people.

Would that be OK? Li argues that even as China and America converge economically and culturally, each society does have a core that remains distinct. Thus someone raised and enculturated in China, even if he moves to America, will remain essentially Chinese, she says: "The basic patterns of cultural learning models are tenacious and unlikely to melt in grand unification." What she doesn't explore as much is what happens when a person is enculturated not in some pure form of Chinese (or Western) culture but in a premelted blend. As I was.

By Jin Li's taxonomy, I am both "European-American" and "Chinese" in my modes of learning. Every item in both columns can apply to me, in different ways at different times. Social science would have predicted this. In responses to psychosocial surveys, Chinese Americans typically land right between people in China and white people in America. But of course, every landing is unique. By Li's taxonomy, my daughter is also a blend of both cultural modes—just not the same blend I am. Olivia, for instance, seems to value "diligence" and "endurance of hardship," whereas I value "active engagement" and "inquiry." So she's more Chinese than me. She also values "personal goals," whereas I perhaps value "contribution to society." So she's more Western than me.

What even the tiny, inconsequential case study of one second-generation man and his third-generation daughter reminds us is this: it is in the blend that the future resides. That blend is not easily put into columns. It is not Eastern or Western. It is just American.

10.

The psychologist Qi Wang has done fascinating cross-cultural research on how mothers speak to their toddlers. Her aim is to understand the impact of mothering styles on the development of a child's autobiographical capacity. In one oft-cited paper, "Sharing Memories and Telling Stories: American and Chinese Mothers and Their 3-Year-Olds," she reported that:

> American mothers and children showed a high-elaborative, independently oriented conversational style in which they co-constructed their memories and stories by elaborating on each other's responses and focusing on the child's personal predilections and opinions. In contrast, Chinese mother-child dyads employed a low-elaborative, interdependently oriented conversational style where mothers frequently posed and repeated factual questions and showed great concern with moral rules and behavioural standards with their children.

Wang also found that the American children, as they grew older, had more elaborate memories of their own childhoods and more recollections of roles and emotions in the stories. The autobiographical memories of the Chinese children were less detailed and focused more on daily routines.

There has not been comparable research done on the styles of Chinese fathers, whether married or divorced, whether in China or in America.

One afternoon when Olivia was nine or ten, I introduced her and her friend to Morse code. They were taken with it immediately. They ran upstairs to a walk-in closet, sitting against opposite walls, and spent the next two hours mastering the alphabet and then tapping encrypted messages to each other in the dark, erupting with satisfied laughter when they'd correctly decoded one.

For a couple of weeks, Olivia and I also tried to converse in Morse. But because my memory is worse than hers, I couldn't keep up. No matter. We moved on to other ways of communicating. All our lives together, we've played with words. Silly ditties improvised during walks and drives. A game called "In my country . . ." where we took turns making up gibberish phrases and "translating" them into English. A cadence call that accompanied my morning push-ups, when she'd lie on my back and count with me. I thought I'd always remember these games and songs. Lately, though, the details have grown blurry. Will my daughter remember? I tell her often about her earliest years and the things we did. I tell her often about my own early years. I tell her about her father's father, and his father too. These things I say expressly. But the prosody of Chinese speech, the topography of Chinese thought, the unity of Chinese sight: these have been sent in code. Will they survive the transmission? Was the signal too tattered? Only her memory will tell.

Epilogue

I ASKED MY MOTHER THE OTHER DAY, WITHOUT WARNING, "Are you American?"

She paused. "I am *Chinese* American," she said. The distinction was this: she still feels too attached to the idea of China, too comfortable with Chinese culture and customs and her Chinese friends and colleagues, to say that she is simply and purely American. But to my mind, her reply (pause included) suggests that she has become simply and purely American.

Julia Liu has now spent many more years of her life in the United States than in China or Taiwan. In the twenty-plus years since my father's death, she has become not only self-sufficient in everyday life but also self-actualized as a citizen. She's come to follow politics and public affairs with a passion. She takes hours to read the *Washington Post* and the local Chinese paper every day. She loves watching Charlie Rose at night and then telling me about the celebrities and politicians who were particularly interesting. She is a choosy independent, watching the debates and candidates closely and casting her vote very deliberately. She joins. She joined her suburban neighborhood association.

She joined Chinese cultural clubs and professional organizations. She joined the alumni associations of her Taiwan high school and college. She joined *my* college alumni association.

These are surface indicia. What marks my mother more deeply as American is that she has made a life that, for better and for worse, could be made only in America. To be purely American is to give oneself over to a jumble of cross-bred influences. To be purely American is to embrace impurity. The dream of claiming this country is not a dream of material advancement only. It is a dream, perhaps more fundamentally, of the freedom to find one's true, self-contradictory self. To contain multitudes and to express them. My mother has been freer to do that in America than she would have been anywhere else on earth. She may feel still as if she is floating between nations. That is what confirms her Americanness.

And this is a time for us all to reconfirm. A generation ago, when Japan's rise seemed to portend America's decline, experts here in business and government sounded an alarm: We needed to act more like the Japanese, they said anxiously, and emulate Japanese ways of running a society. The journalist James Fallows wrote an elegant book in response called *More Like Us*. His point was simple and timeless: America may sometimes falter, but if it simply imitates the competition, it will fail; our best chance for renewal comes from *within*, from embracing the creative disorder that comes with being the world's magnet and mixer of talent and ideas, and keeping channels of opportunity open for all.

Now we live in a time when China is rising and America, at least in relative terms, has lost its dominance. And predictably, experts—not just in business or government but now also in parenting and education and sports—have come to wish that we in America had China's capacity for ruthless efficiency, giant ambition, and hive-minded execution that were all on display, say, during the opening ceremony of the Beijing Olympics.

But we live in a time, too, when Chinese Americans are arriving: in a continuous flow to our shores and into the mainstream of our culture. And the arrival of Chinese Americans is a reminder—is, in fact, proof—that if America wants to sustain its greatness, we need not to emulate China but to be *more like us.* No matter how surpassingly large China's economy becomes, America will always retain an inherent competitive advantage. America, with its recklessly open cultural operating system, is more adaptive to change and diversity than China is; we by character and habit include and combine new genes and memes in a way that China, though modernizing with unprecedented speed, does not. And does not want to.

To put it simply: America makes Chinese Americans, but China does not make American Chinese.

The very idea of an American Chinese—that an American of non-Chinese ancestry might emigrate to China and be able to claim, through residency and mastery of the language and social mores, *Chineseness*—is socially inconceivable there, literally foreign. Imperfect as our union remains, the notion that an immigrant from China might claim Americanness is not only *not* foreign here; it's the *point* of here. To the extent that Chinese Americans thrive, then, America will thrive. To the extent that this country, through the lives of Chinese Americans, can show the world new blended ways of being and thinking, American indispensability will endure. This is our moment, together. Few things today are more American than a Chinese American dream.

Acknowledgments

My agent, Rafe Sagalyn, has been my wise adviser and trusted friend for over twenty years. I feel blessed that he's guided my journey as a writer, and I am proud to be represented so ably by Rafe and the entire team at ICM/Sagalyn.

At PublicAffairs, this book is the result of my collaboration with two fine editors, Brandon Proia and Ben Adams. I'm thankful to Brandon for developing an early idea into a book and to Ben for bringing that idea to fruition. Ben combined a keen eye for detail with a savvy sense of structure, and the manuscript benefited immensely from both. My early rich conversations with Peter Osnos, Clive Priddle, and Susan Weinberg—and my subsequent work with the creative Lindsay Frakoff, Lisa Kaufman, and Jaime Leifer—made me realize that being part of the PublicAffairs family is a privilege. Sandra Beris skillfully steered the production and copyediting process, along with managing editor Melissa Raymond. Designer Pete Garceau created a beautiful cover. I'm so grateful to all of them.

Chris Ader, as always, kept me organized and on schedule, and I'm lucky he was part of my team. Jamin Chen elegantly formatted the two Chinese poems I cite.

So many friends and mentors, over many years of conversations and interactions, shaped the stories and ideas in this book. They know who they are, and I thank them. Parts of this book were developed during a fellowship with the Center for Social Cohesion, a partnership of Zocalo Public Square and Arizona State University, and I thank the CSC team for their support and collaboration. I am very grateful to Gish Jen, Jim Fallows, and Jeff Yang for their support of the book.

Most of all I want to acknowledge my family. My mother, Julia Liu, is my deepest source of inspiration. She gave me feedback the way she does everything—with an open heart and a questioning mind, and with playful seriousness. My partner, Jená Cane (who will be my wife a month after this book is published), pored over every draft. Her instincts, both editorial and emotional, were spot-on and indispensable, and her encouragement carried me through the whole process. My daughter, Olivia Liu, has shaped my writing, my sensibility, and my sense of self even more than is expressed in these pages, and my stepdaughter, Zoey Cane Belyea, has been my creative collaborator in the development of many parts of this book. I am fortunate that these are the women in my life. Finally, I dedicate this book to my father, Chao-hua Liu. He can be found in every page I write.

For Further Reading

Listed here are many of the books that have shaped the ideas and stories in this one. Some I cited or quoted, while others provided background knowledge. This list is by no means intended to be a comprehensive bibliography about Chinese Americans, much less race in America, but I hope it will be useful for readers whose curiosity was sparked by this book.

Baldwin, James. *Nobody Knows My Name.* New York: Vintage, 1982.

———. *Notes of a Native Son.* Boston: Beacon, 1984.

Benedict, Ruth. *Patterns of Culture.* 1st Mariner Books ed. New York: Houghton Mifflin, 2005.

Cain, Susan. *Quiet: The Power of Introverts in a World That Can't Stop Talking.* New York: Crown, 2012.

Chang, Iris. *The Chinese in America: A Narrative History.* New York: Viking, 2003.

Chua, Amy. *Battle Hymn of the Tiger Mother.* New York: Penguin, 2011.

———. *World on Fire: How Exporting Free Market Democracy Breeds Ethnic Hatred and Global Instability.* New York: Anchor Books, 2004.

Confucius. *The Analects.* Translated by D. C. Lau. New York: Penguin, 1987.

Dan, Yu. *Confucius from the Heart.* Translated by Esther Tyldesley. New York: Atria Books, 2006.

Dennerline, Jerry. *Qian Mu and the World of Seven Mansions.* New Haven, CT: Yale University Press, 1988.

Dolin, Eric Jay. *When America First Met China: An Exotic History of Tea, Drugs, and Money in the Age of Sail.* New York: Liveright/Norton, 2012.

Fallows, James. *China Airborne: The Test of China's Future.* New York: Pantheon Books, 2012.

———. *More Like Us.* New York: Houghton Mifflin, 1989.

Fischer, David Hackett. *Albion's Seed: Four British Folkways in America.* New York: Oxford University Press, 1989.

Gabler, Neal. *An Empire of Their Own: How the Jews Invented Hollywood.* New York: Anchor Books, 1989.

Gillenkirk, Jeff, and James Motlow. *Bitter Melon: Inside America's Last Rural Chinese Town.* Berkeley: Heyday Books, 1987.

Gold, Martin. *Forbidden Citizens: Chinese Exclusion and the U.S. Congress: A Legislative History.* Alexandria, VA: TheCapitol .Net, 2012.

Helm, Leslie. *Yokohama Yankee: My Family's Five Generations as Outsiders in Japan.* Seattle: Chin Music, 2013.

Hirsch, E. D., Jr. *Cultural Literacy: What Every American Needs to Know.* New York: Vintage, 1989.

———, Joseph F. Kett, and James Trefil. *The New Dictionary of Cultural Literacy: What Every American Needs to Know.* Completely rev. and updated, 3rd ed. New York: Houghton Mifflin Harcourt, 2002.

Hofstadter, Douglas. *I Am a Strange Loop.* New York: Basic Books, 2008.

Hsieh, Tony. *Delivering Happiness: A Path to Profits, Passion, and Purpose.* New York: Business Plus, 2010.

Huang, Eddie. *Fresh Off the Boat: A Memoir.* New York: Spiegel & Grau, 2013.

Huang, Yunte. *Charlie Chan: The Untold Story of the Honorable Detective and His Rendezvous with American History.* New York: Norton, 2010.

Hwang, David Henry. *Chinglish: A Play.* New York: Theater Communications Group, 2012.

Ignatiev, Noel. *How the Irish Became White.* New York: Routledge, 1995.

Jen, Gish. *Tiger Writing: Art, Culture, and the Interdependent Self.* Cambridge, MA: Harvard University Press, 2013.

Kasinitz, Philip, John H. Mollenkopf, Mary C. Waters, and Jennifer Holdaway. *Inheriting the City: The Children of Immigrants Come of Age.* New York: Russell Sage Foundation, 2008.

Kingston, Maxine Hong. *China Men.* New York: Vintage, 1989.

Kuo, Alex. *A Chinaman's Chance: New and Selected Poems 1960–2010.* La Grande: Wordcraft of Oregon, 2011.

Kwok, Jean. *Girl in Translation.* New York: Riverhead Press, 2011.

Kwong, Peter, and Dusanka Miscevic. *Chinese America: The Untold Story of America's Oldest New Community.* New York: New Press, 2005.

Lai, Him Mark, Genny Lim, and Judy Yung. *Island: Poetry and History of Chinese Immigrants on Angel Island, 1910–1940.* Seattle: University of Washington Press, 1980.

Lakoff, George, and Mark Johnson. *Metaphors We Live By*. Chicago: University of Chicago Press, 1980.

Lee, Wen Ho, with Helen Zia. *My Country Versus Me: The First-Hand Account by the Los Alamos Scientist Who Was Falsely Accused of Being a Spy.* New York: Hyperion, 2001.

Leibovitz, Liel, and Matthew Miller. *Fortunate Sons: The 120 Boys Who Came to America, Went to School, and Revolutionized an Ancient Civilization.* New York: Norton, 2011.

Li, Jin. *Cultural Foundations of Learning: East and West.* New York: Cambridge University Press, 2012.

Lin, Maya. *Boundaries.* New York: Simon & Schuster, 2006.

Link, Perry. *An Anatomy of Chinese: Rhythm, Metaphor, Politics.* Cambridge, MA: Harvard University Press, 2013.

Liu, Dilin. *Metaphor, Culture, and Worldview: The Case of American English and the Chinese Language.* Lanham, MD: University Press of America, 2002.

Liu, Eric. *The Accidental Asian: Notes of a Native Speaker.* New York: Random House, 1998.

———. *Guiding Lights: How to Mentor—and Find Life's Purpose.* New York: Random House, 2004.

———, and Nick Hanauer. *The Gardens of Democracy: A New Story of Citizenship, the Economy, and the Role of Government.* Seattle: Sasquatch Books, 2011.

———, and Nick Hanauer. *The True Patriot: A Pamphlet.* Seattle: Sasquatch Books, 2007.

Liu, Eric, and Scott Noppe-Brandon. *Imagination First: Unlocking the Power of Possibility.* New York: Jossey-Bass, 2011.

Madsen, Richard. *China and the American Dream: A Moral Inquiry.* Berkeley: University of California Press, 1995.

McClain, Charles J. *In Search of Equality: The Chinese Struggle Against Discrimination in Nineteenth-Century America.* Berkeley: University of California Press, 1994.

Ngai, Mae. *Impossible Subjects: Illegal Aliens and the Making of Modern America.* Princeton, NJ: Princeton University Press, 2004.

———. *The Lucky Ones: One Family and the Extraordinary Invention of Chinese America.* New York: Houghton Mifflin, 2010.

Nisbett, Richard. *The Geography of Thought: How Asians and Westerners Think Differently . . . and Why.* New York: Free Press, 2003.

Okihiro, Gary Y. *Margins and Mainstreams: Asians in American History and Culture.* Seattle: University of Washington Press, 1994.

Pfaelzer, Jean. *Driven Out: The Forgotten War Against Chinese Americans.* Berkeley: University of California Press, 2007.

Roth, Philip. *American Pastoral.* New York: Vintage, 1998.
———. *The Plot Against America.* New York: Vintage, 2005.
Seligman, Scott. *The First Chinese American: The Remarkable Life of Wong Chin Foo.* Hong Kong: Hong Kong University Press, 2013.
Smith, Adam. *Theory of Moral Sentiments.* New York: Penguin, 2010.
Spence, Jonathan D. *Chinese Roundabout: Essays in History and Culture.* New York: Norton, 1992.
———. *The Search for Modern China.* New York: Norton, 1990.
Spolin, Viola. *Improvisation for the Theater: A Handbook of Teaching and Directing Techniques.* 3rd ed. Evanston, IL: Northwestern University Press, 1999.
Steele, Claude. *Whistling Vivaldi: How Stereotypes Affect Us and What We Can Do.* New York: Norton, 2010.
Tu, Wei-ming. *Confucian Thought: Selfhood as Creative Transformation.* Albany: State University of New York Press, 1985.
———. *Humanity and Self-Cultivation: Essays in Confucian Thought.* Boston: Cheng & Tsui, 1978.
Wills, Garry. *Inventing America: Jefferson's Declaration of Independence.* New York: Mariner Books, 2002.
Wong, K. Scott. *Americans First: Chinese Americans and the Second World War.* Philadelphia: Temple University Press, 2005.
Wu, Frank. *Yellow: Race in America Beyond Black and White.* New York: Basic Books, 2003.
Yu, Charles. *How to Live Safely in a Science Fictional Universe: A Novel.* New York: Vintage, 2010.

Credits

Excerpt from *Spoken Standard Chinese, Volume One,* by Parker Po-fei Huang and Hugh M. Stimson © 1976, reprinted with permission of Yale University Press.

Excerpt from *Jazz Cliché Capers,* © 1973 by Eddie Harris, reprinted with permission of Seventh House Ltd.

Excerpt from *USA Trilogy,* by John Dos Passos, reprinted with permission of the estate of Lucy Dos Passos. Explore the art and literature of John Dos Passos at www.johndospassos.com.

Excerpt from I*mprovisation for the Theater* ©1963, 1983 by Viola Spolin; ©1999 by Paul Sills and William Sills. All rights reserved.

Excerpt from *Tiger Writing* by Gish Jen, © 2013, originally published by Harvard University Press.

Some passages were adapted from Eric Liu, "The Year of Ming," *Saranac Review,* Fall 2011.

Index

About the Author

Alan Alabastro

ERIC LIU is founder and CEO of Citizen University. He is the author of the New York Times Notable Book *The Accidental Asian: Notes of a Native Speaker; Guiding Lights: How to Mentor—and Find Life's Purpose;* and coauthor, with Nick Hanauer, of *The Gardens of Democracy*. He served as a White House speechwriter for President Bill Clinton and later as the president's deputy domestic policy adviser. He is a columnist for CNN.com and a correspondent for *The Atlantic*. He lives in Seattle with his family. Follow him on Twitter @ericpliu.

PublicAffairs is a publishing house founded in 1997. It is a tribute to the standards, values, and flair of three persons who have served as mentors to countless reporters, writers, editors, and book people of all kinds, including me.

I. F. Stone, proprietor of *I. F. Stone's Weekly*, combined a commitment to the First Amendment with entrepreneurial zeal and reporting skill and became one of the great independent journalists in American history. At the age of eighty, Izzy published *The Trial of Socrates*, which was a national bestseller. He wrote the book after he taught himself ancient Greek.

Benjamin C. Bradlee was for nearly thirty years the charismatic editorial leader of *The Washington Post*. It was Ben who gave the *Post* the range and courage to pursue such historic issues as Watergate. He supported his reporters with a tenacity that made them fearless and it is no accident that so many became authors of influential, best-selling books.

Robert L. Bernstein, the chief executive of Random House for more than a quarter century, guided one of the nation's premier publishing houses. Bob was personally responsible for many books of political dissent and argument that challenged tyranny around the globe. He is also the founder and longtime chair of Human Rights Watch, one of the most respected human rights organizations in the world.

• • •

For fifty years, the banner of Public Affairs Press was carried by its owner Morris B. Schnapper, who published Gandhi, Nasser, Toynbee, Truman, and about 1,500 other authors. In 1983, Schnapper was described by *The Washington Post* as "a redoubtable gadfly." His legacy will endure in the books to come.

Peter Osnos, *Founder and Editor-at-Large*